Essential Speaking Skills

A Handbook for English Language Teachers

Joanna Baker and
Heather Westrup

VSO
Sharing skills
Changing lives

continuum
LONDON • NEW YORK

Continuum

The Tower Building
11 York Road
London SE1 7NX

370 Lexington Avenue
New York
NY 10017–6503

VSO

317 Putney Bridge Road
London
SW15 2PN

First published by Continuum in 2003

British Library Cataloguing-in-Publication Data
A catalogue record for this book is available from the British Library.

ISBN: 0–8264–5844–0 (hardback)
      0–8264–5845–9 (paperback)

Illustrations by Dandi Palmer © VSO/Dandi Palmer

Typeset by Kenneth Burnley, Wirral, Cheshire
Printed and bound in Great Britain by MPG Books Ltd, Bodmin, Cornwall

Contents

Acknowledgements   vi

1. Introduction: The Book and Its Readership   1
2. About Speaking   5
3. Some Possible Barriers to Communication and How to Overcome Them   12
4. A Framework for English Lessons   18
5. Classroom Organization   24
6. Correcting during Speaking Activities   34
7. What Teaching Materials Can We Use?   38
8. Preparing for Speaking: Warmers   45
9. Presenting New Language   56
10. Practising Speaking   67
11. The Production Phase: Speaking Fluently   90
12. Using a Text as a Basis for Speaking Activities   107
13. Pronunciation   124
14. Testing Speaking Skills   144
15. Summary and Ways Forward   155

Index of Activities   157
VSO Books   165
Index   167

Acknowledgements

Many people have contributed to the ideas in this book. In particular, the authors would like to thank VSO and national English language teachers and trainers in Africa, Asia and Europe. Without their creativity and willingness to share their ideas, this book could not have been written.

We should also like to thank the staff of VSO Books for their kind encouragement, co-operation and hard work.

The authors are grateful to Dee Uprichard for permission to reproduce 'Mothering a Mouse' and to G. F. Riaz for 'Shade in Passing'. Every effort has been made to obtain copyright holders' permission and we are sorry if we have not been able to do so in any particular instance. Please send us the relevant information and we shall be happy to include it in the next edition.

1 / Introduction: The Book and Its Readership

1.1 WHO THIS BOOK IS FOR

This is a handbook of practical teaching advice and activities for teachers of English. Its main purpose is to help you improve your students' English speaking skills, whether they are young learners in school, or adult learners in a language class.

The book will also be useful to teacher trainers on both pre-service and in-service courses, curriculum developers and anyone who organizes and plans courses to teach English in schools, colleges or language schools.

Throughout the world today, and especially in developing countries, there is a great need for people to speak English well. In many countries, secondary and higher education is taught in English. Many employers look for good English speakers. So it is important for students to learn to speak English well and for teachers to know how to teach speaking well.

Many teachers are already very good at teaching vocabulary and grammar in order to translate texts and to prepare students for examinations. However, organizing lessons to practise speaking English can be a big challenge for both teachers and students. This handbook can help by giving practical guidance and step-by-step advice. Many teachers teach large classes with few resources: the activities in this book do not require many materials and can be used with large classes.

The advice and activities in this handbook have been contributed by VSO and national English teachers who work in low-resource situations in developing countries worldwide. They have found effective and interesting ways to improve their students' speaking skills.

Whether you have been teaching for many years or are a new teacher, and whether you have classes of 25 or 75 students, you can use the ideas in this book to help your students speak English better both inside and outside the classroom.

1.2 THE CONTENTS OF THIS BOOK

This handbook contains many practical activities for speaking lessons. It also includes advice on how to plan and organize speaking lessons well.

We begin with a look at the importance of speaking and why speaking lessons may differ, depending on where in the world students are learning.

In some classes, students may be very reluctant to speak English. In Section 3, there is a discussion about why students can be shy and we suggest some strategies which you can use to encourage your students to speak in class.

In Section 4, we look at a useful framework for teaching English and for planning and structuring lessons. We suggest how you can incorporate speaking in each lesson, and give practical guidance and ideas on how to organize these lessons. We also explain how to link speaking to the other language skills of listening, reading and writing.

Sections 5, 6 and 7 focus on classroom organization, how you can correct your students during speaking activities and what materials you and your students can use in speaking lessons.

The main part of the book, Sections 8 onwards, includes over 120 activities and variations which we have seen or which have been used by teachers all over the world.

Sections 8 and 9 include ideas for starting lessons and presenting new language through speaking. In Sections 10 and 11, we look at ways of using speaking to practise new vocabulary, grammar or functional language, and practising speaking with different degrees of guidance from the teacher. There are many suggestions for speaking activities in this section.

You may be required to use the texts in your course books as the material for your lessons. So, in Section 12, we show how you can use speaking activities to improve students' understanding and retention of the text.

Section 13 focuses on pronunciation, and includes many different ideas about ways to practise all the elements of this which a good English speaker needs.

Although examinations are often set by ministries and other education institutes, teachers frequently have to set and mark tests for their own students. Section 14 includes some valuable ideas for setting, organizing and marking speaking tests.

1.3 HOW TO USE THIS BOOK

In this book, we use the terms teacher and student, classroom and school. But remember you can also use this book and the activities if you are teaching adult learners.

We suggest that you read Sections 1–7 first. You will then be able to understand which sections will be most useful in your own teaching situation. For example, if you feel your students need a lot of help and guidance during speaking activities, then Section 10 would be most useful for you. But if your students use English outside the classroom and need more practice at speaking fluently, then turn to Sections 11 and 12. If your students have difficulty with pronunciation, Section 13 will help you. If you want ideas for organizing speaking activities to help your students understand and remember text, then turn to Section 14.

Sections 8 onwards contain over 120 activities and variations. We suggest that you start by trying one or two of the short and simple speaking activities with your class. If they work, try others. The activities are not rigid prescriptions, and we hope that you will adapt them and develop other similar activities for your students and teaching context.

Both you and your students may need to become accustomed to new ways of practising and new activities. If speaking practice is new to you and your students, do not expect your students' spoken English to improve in a week or two. As you become more confident, your students will start to enjoy the activities. This will help them to learn well and become more successful in speaking English.

You can use more complex ideas from this book as the year progresses to teach your course or syllabus as your students' English improves.

1.4 WHERE THE IDEAS AND ACTIVITIES COME FROM

Teachers all over the world develop, use and adapt ideas for their classrooms. Many of the practical ideas and activities in this book reflect the learning and experience of VSO teachers and their national colleagues who teach English throughout developing countries and eastern Europe. We have collected teaching ideas from countries including Mongolia, Ethiopia, Pakistan, China, the People's Republic of the Congo and Vietnam. Some ideas are very widely used by teachers so it is difficult to say where the original idea came from, and we are unable to acknowledge the original source.

Many of our colleagues in developing countries work in schools with few resources and some of them teach classes of 100 or more students. The teachers who used and contributed the activities reported that their students' ability to speak English improved considerably. Students enjoyed their English lessons more and became more motivated to learn and to study for their examinations.

We hope this book helps you to use the activities successfully in your own classroom.

2 / About Speaking

In this section, we look at some important issues which surround learning to speak English.

Many teachers worldwide have to teach mainly grammar and vocabulary because these areas are tested in examinations. This means that speaking is a neglected language skill in many classrooms. Students may have a good knowledge of grammar and a wide vocabulary: they can use this knowledge to pass examinations, but they find it more difficult to speak English outside the classroom.

So why is it important for students to learn to speak English, and for teachers to learn to teach speaking?

More and more educators, governments, ministries of education and employers need people who can speak English well. Companies and organizations want staff who can speak English in order to communicate within the international marketplace. Students who can speak English well may have a greater chance of further education, of finding employment and gaining promotion.

Speaking English well also helps students to access up-to-date information in fields including science, technology and health. Good English speakers will be in a strong position to help their country's economic, social and political development. So by learning to speak English well, students gain a valuable skill which can be useful in their lives and contribute to their community and country.

There are also very good educational reasons to practise speaking during a lesson:

► speaking activities can *reinforce* the learning of new vocabulary, grammar or functional language;
► speaking activities give students the chance to *use* the new language they are learning;

▶ speaking activities give more advanced students the chance to *experiment* with the language they already know in different situations and on different topics.

All this helps students to learn English better and succeed in their examinations.

2.2 WHY PRACTISE SPEAKING IN CLASS?

A classroom is not only a place where we learn about the rules of language. It is also a place where students can practise using the language in a supportive environment.

People learn language in different ways. Many people learn to speak English without taking a single lesson. They hear English in their daily lives and have to learn to use English to communicate. In other words, they learn to speak English in the same way as a child learns to speak its first language. But this is a slow process: a child does not usually learn to speak until they are a year old and does not become fluent for several years.

For students who learn English in the classroom, we try to speed up this process. This means that we have to introduce new language and practise it often.

We need to use lots of interesting ways to motivate students to learn and improve. We teach them lots of new words (vocabulary) and tell them how the language is organized (grammar). But we must also give them the opportunity to use and practise the language they have learnt.

2.3 LOOKING AT STUDENTS' NEEDS

In some learning contexts, it is clear why students need to learn to speak English. In many countries, students learn all the other school subjects like maths and science through the medium of English. Secondary-level students or adult learners may be planning to study in an English-speaking country or be preparing for a specific job in their own country. But in other countries, students may not understand why they need to be able to speak English.

How do we motivate these learners? The answer, we believe, lies in making English lessons interesting and lively and giving students a chance to participate in the lessons. If students are interested, they will be more motivated to learn and study well.

Students need to be involved in lessons which use a variety of activities.

Teachers should encourage and support their students, and, if possible, the texts and materials used for teaching should be relevant to the students' needs and to their daily lives. Passing an exam is a very real need, so we have to find ways of studying exam materials in an interesting way.

2.4 WHAT DO WE MEAN BY SPEAKING IN THE CLASSROOM?

In some classrooms, speaking means that the students repeat sentences or dialogues, or chant English words. Repetition is only one useful way of practising new language. It is important for learners to practise the language they are learning in situations which are similar to life outside the classroom. They need to practise real communication:

► talking about their lives;
► talking about news;
► expressing their ideas;
► discussing issues.

When we talk about speaking in this book, we mean using language for a purpose. For example, instead of asking students to repeat sentences, sometimes give students a topic and ask them to construct and say their own responses. In real life, we do not repeat what others say, we make our own sentences and dialogues.

So, teachers need to make time for different kinds of practice, and to think of topics for students to speak about. They also need to create an encouraging environment where students can practise expressing themselves and making themselves understood even if they make mistakes. This type of speaking practice prepares them for using English outside the classroom.

This book will help you to plan lessons which include plenty of speaking practice.

2.5 ACCURACY AND FLUENCY

Someone who can use English well is usually both accurate and fluent. Accurate speakers do not make mistakes in grammar, vocabulary or pronunciation. Fluent speakers can express themselves appropriately and without hesitation. Fluent speakers do not usually worry unduly about making mistakes.

In a language lesson, students need to spend time on becoming more accurate. But they also need to practise using the language fluently. The amount of time spent on each skill will be different in each learning situation. Also, as we shall see in Section 4, an activity which starts with an emphasis on accuracy will often give students the chance to practise speaking fluently later in the lesson.

The learning context plays a large role in determining what is appropriate for students. Students who have to pass traditional examinations based on a knowledge of good vocabulary and grammar will need to spend a lot of time learning to use the language accurately. Others may need to spend most of the lesson doing activities to practise using the English they have learned in a much freer way.

2.6 DIFFERENT LEARNING CONTEXTS

In some countries, learners need to use English in their everyday lives. They also see and hear English every day. In this situation, learners have a lot of practice outside the classroom, and they often learn to speak a certain amount of English in quite a short time. If they go to English classes, each of them will know some different language because they have different knowledge and different life experiences in English outside the classroom. The teacher knows this and can organize lessons which practise not only the language taught in the classroom, but all the language which the students have learned from their lives outside school.

However, in many other parts of the world, learners:

▶ never hear English spoken except by their teacher;
▶ never read English except in their English textbook;
▶ never expect to use much English outside the classroom.

In some cases, the teacher may not be confident in speaking English and may use the local language most of the time in the classroom.

Some students work very hard because they hope that speaking English well will lead to a better job when they leave school. But many younger students may not understand why they should learn English, so their motivation may be very low. In some countries, parents send their children to extra lessons. They hope their children will work in an international business or will study abroad. These parents are highly motivated but sometimes their children are not. Young children are sometimes tired and find it difficult to concentrate on extra tutorials after a day at school.

It is very important for lessons to be interesting and to contain varied activities to give students, particularly younger ones, as much encouragement as possible. Students need to participate actively and to enjoy their English

ABOUT SPEAKING / 9

classes. Even in large classes, where there are few resources and space is limited, it is possible to do useful activities. This book contains many such activities which have been used successfully by teachers facing similar challenges. They show that teachers in different learning situations can organize lessons which motivate their students and give them the best possible chance of improving their spoken English.

2.7 DIFFERENT TYPES OF LEARNERS

Adult learners

Adult beginners have specific learning characteristics which need to be taken into account when planning their language learning.

Adult language learners who are beginners:

- ▶ may have been away from formal education for a long time;
- ▶ may have fixed ideas about how to learn;
- ▶ are often highly motivated;
- ▶ have specific and immediate language needs;
- ▶ sometimes need to learn the Roman script;
- ▶ often have high expectations of their learning;
- ▶ need fast progress;
- ▶ are sometimes shy about showing their lack of English;
- ▶ are easily frustrated.

Once we understand these characteristics, we need to adapt our teaching in the following ways:

- ▶ simplify our language to talk about adult ideas;
- ▶ use many different teaching methods which respond to different learning strategies;
- ▶ teach in logical steps;
- ▶ plan lots of recycling of new language with different activities;
- ▶ plan specific language goals;
- ▶ teach specific language skills;
- ▶ do lots of work on pronunciation, as previous errors can be difficult to change;
- ▶ help students learn lots of vocabulary;
- ▶ encourage students to do homework and self study.

Most of the activities in this book can be adapted for adult beginners.

Young learners

Young learners, too, have special characteristics. Many of these mean that they are very likely to be good learners of a new language, because:

► they are often enthusiastic and inquisitive;
► they are not self-conscious;
► they have not yet developed fixed learning patterns;
► they are often good mimics (good at imitating sounds and intonation);
► they often have a good imagination;
► they like to play the same games and hear the same stories over and over again;
► they respond to language by what they can *do* with it, and do not worry about individual words or sentence structure.

Other characteristics which we should take into account are:

► they learn best through the five senses – sight, touch, hearing, smell and taste;
► they may not yet be able to read their own language;
► they have a short attention span, often as little as five minutes;
► they are often very physical and need to be active;
► they have a natural interest in new things.

So when we think of how young learners should best learn a language, we must remember to:

► keep activities short;
► use lots of pictures or real objects;
► if possible, let them move around during or between activities;
► use lots of repetition in songs and action rhymes;
► emphasize speaking over writing;
► include plenty of variety.

Which language should teachers use with young learners?

Many teachers of young children are not specialists at teaching English and feel uncertain about their ability to speak English themselves in the classroom. However, it is a good habit to try to use as much English as possible during lessons, so that children have the chance of hearing it. Understanding instructions in English is a useful skill for when they are older. Look at Section 5.8, page 31, for more tips on how to start using English more in the classroom.

Throughout this book, you will find reference to materials and activities which are suitable for younger learners. By using these, you will ensure that younger children have a very good chance of becoming confident and competent users of English at an early age.

3 / Some Possible Barriers to Communication and How to Overcome Them

There are many reasons why students may find learning and using English difficult. This can lead to real barriers to communication, and can contribute to poor motivation in learning.

If you teach young learners, you will probably find that they do not have any lasting barriers to communication. This is because most of them are willing to speak to other students in their class. Also, they do not have much knowledge of the outside world which could negatively affect their learning style, learning ability and interest in learning.

In this section, we look at some of the more fundamental and long-lasting barriers to communication. We also suggest ways of overcoming these barriers so you can help your students communicate more easily and more successfully.

3.1 CULTURAL DIFFERENCES

The social roles and rules for speaking can be different in each culture. These social rules have a strong effect on a learner's interest and ability to learn to speak in a foreign or second language.

For example, in all cultures, a speaker's social status, sex, age and level of education may affect the language, specific words and level of formality they use. There may be social rules for when and how we speak to someone, or when and how someone speaks to us, who speaks first and who finishes the conversation.

In some cultures, students are not expected to speak until they are asked to do so by the teacher. This makes it more difficult for students to practise conversation. Teachers who work in their own country or community will know about local customs and expectations. However, teachers working in a different community or country will need to find out this information by asking local teachers and other people in the community.

Barriers to learning can occur if students knowingly or unknowingly transfer the cultural rules from their mother tongue to a foreign language. Students may fear causing offence by what they say in a foreign language, and this makes them unwilling to speak. Teachers need to become aware of the social and linguistic rules and roles in their culture, as well as the social and linguistic rules and roles of English: for example, acceptable ways of taking turns in conversation or ways of interrupting other speakers. You need to teach these rules and roles to help your students to use appropriate cultural and linguistic behaviour.

3.2 PERSONAL DIFFERENCES

Our ability to learn a new language and succeed in language learning also depends on the type of learner we are. Some people are naturally happy to try anything new and are not afraid to make mistakes, while others are afraid of new situations.

If you introduce students to new learning habits and new learning activities over a few weeks or months, you can help them overcome fears or doubts that they may have about learning a new language.

Help your language learners become more self-aware by:

► encouraging them to think about how they feel about language learning;
► asking them to think about how they feel about learning English;
► asking them how they think they will use English in their future life;
► finding out what they know about how English is used in different countries.

Ask students to think about what kind of speaker they are in their mother tongue. If students are confident and fluent in their mother tongue, then they are more likely to become confident second-language learners. Similarly, students who are shy and hesitant speakers in their mother tongue are more likely to be shy and hesitant speakers in a foreign language.

However, some language learners develop different speaking characteristics in a foreign language. Some confident speakers may find it difficult when they realize they are not as fluent as they would like to be in a foreign language. These learners may become shy and hesitant. On the other hand, shy speakers may find they can hide their shyness when they speak a foreign language. So, knowing what kind of language learner we are can help explain our performance in learning a foreign language. This self-knowledge may help language learners to focus on areas they need to work on.

3.3 DEALING WITH A LACK OF CONFIDENCE

Language learners have to expect that some people, both in and out of the classroom, may be unwilling to listen or to help when they try to communicate in a new language. Their requests or questions may be misunderstood. This may result in a friendly joke but it could also end in a situation where students become embarrassed and are not sure how to continue. However, even in their first language, students may sometimes face situations where they lose confidence.

You can help to prepare your students for new and unexpected situations. For example, you can ask them to write down briefly what they want to say, and then read it aloud. Although this is not 'real', spontaneous speaking, it is reassuring for students to be able to prepare what they want to say. This activity helps them to use more correct English and can give them the confidence to speak without reading their notes later.

You need to help students feel that they:

► are learning in a supportive atmosphere;
► are free to ask when they do not understand something;
► can ask questions;
► are not afraid of making mistakes, because making mistakes is part of the learning process. We learn from our mistakes.

So you need to give your students lots of praise, because all speakers need to know that their communication is acknowledged and that they have been understood.

You can create a supportive atmosphere by reducing the risk of students making mistakes. We can improve students' motivation by allowing them time to prepare before they have to speak. In this way, students do not feel pressured to say something until they have had time to think about it.

Ensure that you give enough time for students to practise new language in a variety of ways and in a step-by-step process. Language learners can be nervous about speaking to the teacher in front of the whole class, so you can practise in the security of pairs and groups, where learners need not fear being heard by the whole class, or be afraid of being constantly corrected. This means students are more likely to say something correctly, which can make them feel more confident. It also gives all the learners in the class maximum practice, as they are all speaking at the same time. In this way, teachers can help students who are not very confident to become more successful speakers of English.

3.4 DEALING WITH A BIG CHALLENGE

When we start learning a new language, if we are lucky, we are taught in small and guided steps. But many language learners find that there is too much to remember and too much to understand. It can seem like a big challenge to reach the stage at which communication becomes easier and more useful.

Many language learners go through this stage several times. Some important points to remember are to:

▶ teach a little new language at a time;
▶ explain new ideas and new language clearly and simply;
▶ encourage students to ask questions;
▶ avoid asking, 'Do you understand?', as you may not get a true response (it is easy for students to reply 'Yes', even if they do not understand!);
▶ revise recently learnt language often;
▶ help students learn with a variety of learning activities.

3.5 NO TIME FOR SPEAKING WHEN STUDYING FOR EXAMINATIONS

Most schools and many language institutes aim to help their students pass local, national or international examinations. Many of these examinations are written, with little or no speaking element to them. Teachers (and students) may feel that speaking skills can be ignored because it is much more important to improve writing skills for the examination. It is also easier to correct mistakes in written work, and teachers and students can more easily see their progress, or lack of it, in writing. Speaking can be more difficult to mark as correct or wrong.

However, speaking practice can assist students in learning vocabulary and grammar. Improving these will help students improve their writing skills. So, in the end, speaking practice can help written work and written examinations. And once students have passed the exam, they will have the useful skill of being able to speak English, not just write answers to questions.

3.6 PREPARATION FOR SPEAKING

Many students find it difficult to respond if the teacher asks them to say something in a foreign language. They may have little idea about what to say, they may not know the words to use, or they may not be sure how to use the grammar.

When students write, they have time to sit and think about what they will write, and how they will write it. But in speaking, they have to respond more quickly. This can make students afraid to say anything!

In this book, we show how you can prepare students for speaking in class. This involves teaching and practising the words and grammar that the students will need for the speaking activity. For example, if the speaking activity is about buying food in the market, learners need to know the English words for fruit and vegetables, some key questions, such as 'Can I have . . . ?' and 'How much is . . . ?', and to understand the words for prices and numbers. If you prepare your students before they do a speaking activity, they will find conversations easier.

Teachers also need to allow silence. In our mother tongue, we are happy to have silence sometimes. When we are speaking to someone, we need spaces to think about what we have heard and what we are going to say. Encourage students not to be nervous if they have to take a little time to think between sentences. Hesitating and rephrasing words halfway through a sentence is a normal part of speaking. Students need to know how to use the hesitation sounds of 'mmm' and 'errr'. These useful 'fillers' give speakers a little more time to think before speaking.

3.7 INTEREST IN THE TOPIC

Students find it difficult to have a conversation on a topic that they know little about. So if you ask primary pupils to talk about going to the bank or checking in at the airport, you may find that they cannot do it successfully. You need to give them topics that they know about, or would like to know about. If you have to follow your course book, you can adapt the topics if necessary. For example, if the topic in the course book is 'Buying a car', you can change it to 'Buying food' or 'Buying clothes'. If you are not sure, ask your class what topics interest them.

If students are learning a language that is not used in their everyday life, they can easily feel that there is no real need for them to learn to say anything in the foreign language. If this is the case, then you need to make the language lesson fun to motivate students to speak. Learning with fun means that students take a more active part in the lesson, and involves teaching and learning through a variety of interesting and guided learning activities. In the following sections, you will find many ways to do this.

4 / A Framework for English Lessons

In this section, we look at several ways of organizing a lesson so that students practise speaking. This helps students to use the new language they have learnt and to speak English more confidently in a wide variety of situations.

The way the lesson progresses differs according to how much English the students know or how much English they see, hear and use outside the classroom. However, the final objective of a speaking lesson is always to help students speak English more confidently in a wide variety of situations.

Let's look at some ways of organizing lessons.

A useful framework for organizing lessons is the PPP or 'Presentation, Practice and Production' model. PPP is particularly effective for lower levels and where students have little input apart from their teacher and course books.

In PPP, language is divided into distinct parts: grammar, vocabulary and functional language. Functional language is a way of describing what we *do* with the language, for example:

► giving information: 'I go to school by bus';
► asking for advice: 'What do you think I should do?'.

In a lesson, we might choose to teach a tense, information about adjectives, for example, a collection of new words or some phrases to express a language function. We call these the language items or target language. The language item is usually introduced at the beginning of the lesson. During the lesson, students practise this new language in different ways together with the language that they already know.

Let's look at each phase.

Presentation phase

At the beginning of the lesson, the teacher presents or teaches the new language to the students. In this phase, the teacher will probably be more active than the students, although the teacher can ask them questions to find out what they already know. Teachers also sometimes ask students to guess meanings of words or details of a grammatical structure. We call these techniques elicitation. Elicitation helps to keep students involved during the Presentation phase.

Practice phase

Once students understand the meaning and use of the new language and know how it should be pronounced, they need to practise using it correctly. At first, the teacher needs to organize very controlled activities like class repetition (drilling). This gives the students lots of support and makes sure that they can reproduce the language accurately. Students may also do short written exercises to reinforce their learning. Later in the Practice phase, the teacher introduces less controlled activities, which only guide the students while they practise. Students can then work without the support of the teacher in the next phase, the Production phase.

Production phase

Students should now be able to use the new language appropriately and accurately. In the Production phase, the teacher organizes activities for the students in which they can use the new language they have just learnt and any other language they already know. They will probably work in pairs or groups on activities, such as a discussion, a role play or solving a problem. During this phase, students use any language they know. There is little direction from the teacher because the focus is on fluency and errors are not so important. The Production phase is sometimes also called the free phase or the fluency phase. This is the phase which most resembles the use of language in real life outside the classroom.

4.3 WHY THE PPP FRAMEWORK IS USEFUL AND EFFECTIVE

The PPP framework is a flexible format. The three phases can be fitted into one lesson period, or you can plan a whole series of lessons on a PPP framework. In this case, the Presentation and Practice phases might take one or two lessons, and the Production phase might last several lessons, for example, if it is a long role play or a series of presentations by students.

If your students have a high level of English, another possibility is to start with the Production phase. Students may already know a lot of grammar and vocabulary and may need practice in using it in less structured activities. In this case, you monitor the speaking activity carefully, dealing with errors and sorting out any difficulties later, even sometimes going back to a brief presentation phase and practice phase if needs be. Section 6 tells you more about how to correct during the Production phase of the lesson.

Sometimes, students will do speaking activities which will help them learn new grammar, vocabulary or functional language, and sometimes the objective of the lesson will be solely to help students improve their skill at speaking. A PPP framework can be used as a basis for both these types of lesson.

There are many different methods of teaching English. In many countries, students learn by remembering a lot of vocabulary and learning to understand the grammar of English. This is very useful when they have to translate texts from one language to another or write essays, but it does not give them the chance to communicate through speaking. Other students learn through oral repetition of set phrases, but this too has its limitations when students need to use English outside the classroom.

A PPP framework incorporates the most effective parts of these and other methods. It is simple, easy to use and very adaptable. Teachers can start by using a simple model of the three Ps and later they can build on the framework as they grow in experience and confidence.

4.4 INTEGRATING THE LANGUAGE SKILLS

In a PPP framework, all four language skills (speaking, listening, reading, writing) can be used to practise the new target language. A sample lesson might look like the example in Figure 4.1.

Even if the focus of the lesson is on speaking practice alone, listening is closely linked to speaking. Writing and reading can easily and naturally be incorporated into the lesson. This is much the same as in our real lives, where the four skills are constantly linked.

Here are some examples:

Mary wants to speak to Grace on the telephone. Grace is not at home. Mpenza takes the call and writes a note for Grace. (Speak – listen – write)

	Teacher activity	Student activity	Skill
Presentation phase	Presents new language	Watch and listen	Listening
	Elicits new language	Listen and **speak**	Listening **Speaking**
	Presents new language through text	Read	Reading
Practice phase	Models language	Repeat	**Speaking**
	Gives written exercise	Read and write	Reading and writing
Production phase	Sets up fluency activity	Discuss in groups	**Speaking**
	Monitors group work	Records results of discussion	Writing
	Watches	Present work to others	**Speaking**

Figure 4.1: Example of language skills in a PPP lesson

Luis (a teacher) gives a lecture. Elena (a student) takes notes. José (another student) is ill and misses the lecture. Elena tells José about the contents of the lecture. (Speak – listen – write – speak – listen)

Sita reads some useful information in a magazine. Sita tells Nusrat about it. Nusrat writes to the magazine for details. Nusrat reads the response when it comes and tells Sita more about it. (Read – speak – listen – write – read – speak)

Minh (the boss) gives instructions to Kwan (her assistant). Kwan listens and does what he is asked to do. (Speak – listen – do)

Yuri and Piotr are students. They have been given some written instructions about the work they have to do. Piotr has lost his instructions and telephones Yuri. So Yuri tells Piotr what he has to do. (Read – speak – listen – do)

Phase of the lesson:	Controlled practice (Practice phase)
Level:	Class 3a (42 students) Elementary
Language needed:	Do you have any . . . ? Yes, I do/No I don't. How much do . . . cost? They cost . . . dollars. Numbers
Materials:	Two posters, one with a shopping list, one with a list of items at the market stall
Grouping:	Students work in pairs
Time:	5–10 minutes
Instructions:	Explain the activity to students (in the students' first language). Write a short shopping list and short list of items at the market stall on the board and demonstrate the activity with Stephan or Lisa. Put students into pairs side by side and tell one of the pair to turn and face the wall at the far end of the room. Put up one poster at each end of the room. Ask one pair to demonstrate the activity using these posters. Then ask pairs to practise quietly all at the same time.
Follow-up:	Ask pairs to make their own shopping lists and lists of items at the stall and practise the activity again. They should not show each other their lists.

Figure 4.2: Example of part of a lesson plan based on variation 2 of activity 28, information gap drill (page 72)

All these examples can be used as activities in the classroom, and in this book we shall suggest ways of following up speaking activities with different activities using the other language skills.

4.5 USING THE ACTIVITIES IN THIS BOOK

Sections 8–13 in this book include many activities for the different phases of a PPP lesson. There are step-by-step instructions on how to set up and organize the activity with your students, and there are suggestions of how the activity can be used at different levels and with different language areas. You might find it useful to make a little individual plan such as the example in Figure 4.2 to help you ensure that you are well prepared to do the activity with your students. This would only be part of your overall lesson plan.

5 / Classroom Organization

Effective classroom organization is important. It can help make your job easier and can help students to learn to speak. Good classroom organization can help you to:

► keep everyone's attention;
► deal with students who have a range of abilities and learning styles;
► encourage weaker students;
► avoid discipline problems.

There are lots of 'little answers' which can help classroom organization. Some of these suggestions may work for you and your students, so try them. You may need to adapt a suggestion so that it will work better in your classroom.

Young learners have a short attention span, and they need a lot of variety with short learning activities. However they can easily become over-excited by moving around the classroom for too long. So it is a good idea to alternate moving-about activities with quieter activities, such as listening to a story or drawing. Young learners are often easier to manage and they are usually happy to be told what to do, but you need to make class rules clear and you need to apply them with care.

5.1 THE TEACHER'S ROLE IN SPEAKING LESSONS

The more time you speak during the lesson, the less time there is for your students to speak. So, to help your students speak, you need to have several different roles. A teacher is a giver of information and a corrector of mistakes. But in addition, at different times during the lesson, the teacher can also be a model, a prompt, an organizer, an encourager and a monitor. These roles can help you to manage the lesson and help the students learn.

You are a *model* in the Presentation phase, when students are aiming for accuracy. You say new language and ask students to repeat until they are correct and confident with their pronunciation of the new language.

You are a *prompt* during the Practice phase, encouraging students to think about how to use the new language they are learning.

During the Production phase, you are *organizer, encourager* and *monitor* as students work in pairs or groups to practise fluency. You need to organize the groups, encourage students who may be afraid of making mistakes or who may not know exactly what to say, and be a monitor to keep the noise at an acceptable level and to make sure that everyone is doing what they are supposed to be doing.

5.2 PLANNING AND ORGANIZATION

Classroom organization is an important part of teaching, particularly when students are speaking in pairs or groups. If you can manage the pairs or groups well, and organize the speaking activities carefully, you and your students can enjoy and learn from their speaking lessons.

Careful planning keeps all students involved in the lesson and allows them to work with each other. You do not give up control during any part of the lesson, but during pair work and group work, you manage and monitor the students differently.

When you plan lessons, here are some areas you should think about in detail:

► exactly what kind of speaking practice will the students do?
► how much will you speak and how much will your students speak?
► what different activities will you use?
► when will the students work in pairs or groups, and how will you group them?
► how much time will each part of the lesson take?
► what will you do if the lesson turns out to be too easy or too difficult?
► how will you assess the success of the lesson?

Look back to page 18 to remind yourself of the place of speaking in a lesson, and for a brief overview of the useful PPP lesson format.

5.3 SETTING UP ROUTINES AND SIGNALS TO HELP WITH GOOD CLASSROOM ORGANIZATION

You need to teach your class some simple but important routines and signals which can make changes during the lesson easier and faster.

Make sure students can see you and hear your instructions easily to avoid discipline problems. However, avoid shouting because it does not help reduce noise. Instead:

► check that your students have understood by asking them questions about the new information;
► ask some students to tell you about something they have learnt in their own words;
► use your students' first language sometimes to make information and instructions clearer.

Students usually respond better if you use their names. So whether you are praising or disciplining someone, try and use their name if possible. At the beginning of a new term and particularly if you have a large class, getting to know all the names takes a bit of time. Try drawing all the desks on a piece of paper and writing each student's name in the correct place. Keep this on your desk to help you remember.

Another way to make the classroom more manageable is to set up your own rules. Discuss these rules with your students and then ask them to write the agreed rules on a poster which everyone can see. For example, you need some rules for when to speak English, how to enter and leave the classroom, when you expect homework to be done and how it is to be given in.

If you ask for or choose classroom monitors, you can gain some help with daily and time-consuming tasks. Most students like being a monitor, particularly if you present the job as being something special, or as a reward for improving work or behaviour.

These ideas should make maintaining discipline a bit easier. Remember: keeping all your students busy and interested prevents discipline problems.

It is very important that you can achieve and maintain silence for discipline or learning. You need to teach your students the signal that means you want them to stop what they are doing, stop talking and look at and listen to you. One way to do this is to stand quietly with your arm up, or to tap gently on the board. You do not need to say anything, but look around the room until everyone has noticed you are signalling for silence. Shouting at students to be quiet does not usually work.

5.4 WHOLE-CLASS WORK, PAIR WORK AND GROUP WORK

Let's look at three different teaching and learning interactive patterns: whole-class work, pair work and group work.

Whole-class work is when you teach the whole class at the same time. You probably do most of the talking, and your students sit quietly, listen to you, answer your questions, or read or write. This whole-class teaching situation is useful for certain stages of a lesson. It is often done in the Presentation phase, or when you begin a new topic. Remember that even if all your students are sitting quietly, they may not be paying attention, so make sure that you speak distinctly, give clear instructions and involve the students at every opportunity.

Pair work and group work involve all the students in the class working at the same time. The important difference between whole-class work and pair and group work is that the students work with each other, and their attention is not focused on the teacher. You have different, guiding roles during this type of activity, which we look at in more detail later in this section.

Pair work and group work are important because they:

▶ give all students lots of speaking practice;
▶ allow the quieter or weaker students to speak to another student, instead of speaking in front of the whole class;
▶ teach students to help each other with their learning.

Working in pairs and groups, students can talk about their own ideas, opinions and real-life facts and situations, and develop real spoken communication skills.

Introducing your students to pair work and group work

Pair work or group work may be new for you and your students. You may think that these ways of learning are not 'real' learning, and that they can be noisy and time-consuming. But if activities are well planned and controlled, pair and group work are good ways to improve students' speaking skills, particularly in a class with a range of mixed abilities.

Group work is an extension of pair work, so if you have not done group work before, we suggest you try pair work first. When you and your students are more confident working like this, you can then move on to group work, in small groups of up to six.

Here are the important points to remember about pair and group work:

▶ explain to your students why pair and group work are a good idea;
▶ present new language and practise it with the whole class first;
▶ explain carefully what you want the pairs or groups to do, and write the instructions on the board;

▶ demonstrate the activity in front of the whole class with a student who is confident and who speaks good English;

▶ demonstrate with one pair of students standing up, and ask the rest of the class to watch and listen;

▶ form the pairs or groups, then ask students to speak quietly, otherwise the noise level will be too high;

▶ if your classroom has furniture fixed to the floor, you can ask students to turn and face the person sitting to the left or to the right of them. Groups of four students can be formed by asking alternate pairs to turn round and face the pair sitting behind them;

▶ tell students not to worry about making mistakes;

▶ tell students how long they have for the activity and signal the start of the activity;

▶ move away from the centre front of the classroom;

▶ watch and listen, and note down problems and common mistakes;

▶ signal the end of the activity and gain everyone's attention;

▶ give or ask for appropriate feedback.

Here are some ways in which you can quickly and easily form the new interaction patterns:

▶ use your hands to indicate clearly which pairs or groups will be working together;

▶ ask students to take turns and call out the numbers 1, 2, 3 or 4 around the whole class. Then ask each set of 1s, 2s, 3s and 4s to work as a group;

▶ if you have space for movement in your classroom, you could ask students to call out 1, 2, 3, or 4 in order. Then ask all the 1s to work as a group, all the 2s to work as a group, and so on;

▶ you can make groups as small as three students, and ideally a maximum of five students (groups of more than five often find it hard to work well together).

If you find that your students are particularly resistant to pair or group work, you may need several weeks or even months to slowly train them. Continue using short, simple activities to help them gain confidence gradually.

Managing the introduction of group and pair work in your school

You may hear questions and doubts from school principals, other teachers, inspectors and parents when you introduce any new ways of teaching. This can be because many people are more accustomed to students who sit quietly, listen to the teacher and take notes. Some people may not understand why you are asking the students to participate in lessons by asking them questions and asking them to work and talk with each other. Therefore it is very important to tell everyone involved in your school what you are doing in lessons and why you are introducing some changes. You can do this by speaking to your colleagues, in a letter, on a poster or through a short talk. You could also invite people to observe a lesson so that they can see for themselves what is happening in your class.

If parents, school principals or other teachers challenge you about the higher noise level, you can explain what the students are doing and why it is important. Tell them that you are still in charge, but with a different kind of control.

If your students are accustomed to sitting quietly in rows and listening to the teacher, then the idea of working in pairs or groups can seem strange and difficult to them, too. So when you introduce pair or group work for the first time, you need to explain why they are going to work in a different way, and that you are asking them to work with each other to practise speaking. In pair work and group work, we can encourage peer teaching, which means classmates helping each other to understand and learn something new.

5.5 RESPONSIBILITIES WITHIN GROUPS

During group work, encourage your students to take some responsibility for doing the activity properly. This will help them gain confidence and develop their speaking skills. This responsibility involves making sure that:

▶ everyone knows what to do;
▶ everyone knows how they are going to do it;
▶ everyone takes turns at speaking, and they do not all talk at the same time;
▶ everyone who wants to speak has a chance to do so;
▶ everyone knows what has been said at the end of the activity;
▶ someone is able to report what their group talked about.

Different group activities require different jobs to be done. For example:

▶ a text needs to be handed out to students before they can begin the speaking activity;
▶ some information needs to be exchanged between groups at a certain stage;
▶ notes need to be taken about what has been said.

One good way to ensure that these tasks happen is for students in the groups to have specific roles, or a specific piece of work to do. If you give students this level of responsibility, you may find it easier to manage the activity, even in a large class. Here are some roles that members of the group can be given, or choose to take:

▶ the secretary listens and makes notes as necessary;
▶ the leader decides who speaks next;
▶ the presenter talks to other groups or to the whole class;
▶ the monitor checks that (correct) English is used.

However, try not to give the same role to the same student in every lesson, and make sure that everyone has a chance to have at least one of these roles every week. Sometimes, it is helpful to give roles such as leader or monitor to quiet or shy students, as it can give them confidence to have to say a few words. Similarly, talkative and confident students can be diverted from dominating the talk by giving them roles such as secretary or presenter.

5.6 DEALING WITH NOISE

Fluency speaking activities can be noisy, but there is a difference between 'naughty noise' when students are getting out of control, and 'busy noise' when groups and pairs are talking at the same time. You need to encourage students working in groups to talk quietly (see below for some ideas).

In the classroom it is important to be able to distinguish between naughty noise and busy noise. Naughty noise is disruptive, and this usually means that:

▶ the work is too easy;
▶ the work is too difficult;
▶ the work is not very interesting;
▶ your students have not understood what to do;
▶ some students have finished their work.

In all these situations, students may start talking in their first language or behaving disruptively.

Even if you have prepared the lesson well, the noise level may become too high, particularly if pairs or groups are working hard on an interesting activity. The class next door or the school principal might complain if you do not deal with this situation quickly. One way to reduce busy noise is simply to gain the attention of the class and ask them to speak more quietly. Or you can teach the students that when you give a particular signal, for example, raise your arm or clap your hands, you want silence.

5.7 VARYING THE INTERACTION PATTERNS AND LEARNING ACTIVITIES

All lessons need to include a good variety of interaction patterns and learning activities. This variety can help keep students involved, interested and motivated to learn.

Variety of interaction patterns and learning activities also gives all your students a chance to benefit. All learners need a part of each lesson which they will enjoy or excel at, as they have different ways of learning and different interests and skills.

Ways to vary the interaction patterns and learning activities include:

► using a variety of Presentation, Practice and Production techniques and activities;
► how much student participation you use;
► how much you use students' ideas, opinions and experiences;
► how much and what kind of pair and group work there is;
► how much language is cued from words, gesture or pictures;
► varying the teaching aids you use;
► how much correction there is, when the correction is done, and who does the correction;
► how you encourage contributions from students who are not the quickest, loudest or the best in class;
► what type of feedback there is, and who gives the feedback.

5.8 SOME HELPFUL LANGUAGE TEACHERS CAN USE

Many teachers feel uncertain about their own ability to speak English in the classroom. However, it is a good idea to use as much English as possible during lessons, as this may be the only chance students have to hear the language.

You can begin by learning a few simple instructions, and then gradually build on these. Write simple phrases on a piece of paper, and refer to them during the lesson. Some important words and phrases are shown in Figure 5.2.

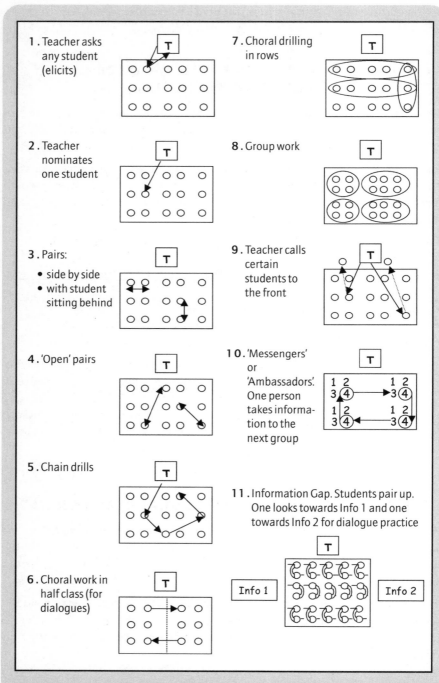

Figure 5.1: Classroom interaction patterns: whole-class work, pair work and group work

> ► Listen.
> ► Look at me.
> ► Are you ready?
> ► Have you finished?
> ► Everyone say it.
> ► Repeat.
> ► Again.
> ► What's this?
> ► Stop now.
> ► Come here.
> ► Copy this.
> ► Put away your books.
> ► That's all for today.

Figure 5.2: Useful phrases for teachers

If your students do not understand much English, start by giving instructions in their first language, followed immediately by the same phrase in English. Later you can start with English followed by their language, and when your students understand English better, use English alone. You can then slowly start using more instructional phrases, using the same process.

6 / Correcting during Speaking Activities

In this section, we look at different ways of correcting during speaking lessons.

Some teachers and many learners think that their spoken English will improve if someone corrects them all the time. But learners can find this very demotivating and become afraid to speak. In fact, students are learning when they make mistakes or correct others, so correction should always be done positively and with encouragement. There are many ways to correct errors and you can help your students by choosing the right way to correct for the different parts of a lesson.

Let students know when you expect them to be accurate and when you want them to practise becoming more fluent. This way, they will soon learn why you correct them some times and not others. They will come to recognize the phases of a lesson and understand your principles of correction.

6.1 WHEN TO CORRECT

You will remember that in a lesson based on a PPP framework, there is a strong focus on accuracy during the Presentation and Practice phases. During this time, you will correct all the errors of grammar, vocabulary and pronunciation. Later in the Practice phase, when you are guiding rather than controlling the activities, you will continue to correct occasionally, when students are still making mistakes in the language they have just learned. In the Production phase, when students are practising fluency, you should not correct them, but note errors and correct the students after the activity or at the beginning of the next lesson.

6.2 WHO SHOULD CORRECT?

In most classrooms, you have to let the students know when there is an error. You can then either give a correct version which students repeat, or you can help students to correct themselves. Invite other students to try to spot errors and to give a correct version. In a classroom where the atmosphere is one of encouragement and co-operation, this is quite possible, although it may take a little time for students to take on this role.

When you are correcting, try to avoid saying 'no' or 'that's wrong', and instead use phrases like 'nearly', or 'not quite', or 'that's a good idea, but not right'. When the student does repeat a word or phrase perfectly, remember to give genuine praise: 'well done', or 'that's it', or 'excellent'.

Encourage students to try to correct themselves or each other (self or peer correction) by asking the class questions (see below for questioning techniques). In this way, students are always involved in the learning process. They are also working towards the time when they use English in real life and there is no longer a teacher to correct them.

6.3 WAYS OF CORRECTING DURING THE PRACTICE PHASE

Letting students know that an error has occurred

You can:

▶ repeat the error with a questioning look (head on one side, eyebrows raised);
▶ repeat the phrase as far as the error and then pause, silently inviting students to try to finish it correctly.

Helping students to correct themselves and others

Remember to:

▶ ask students 'Is that correct?', 'Do you think that's correct?', or even 'Do you like that?';
▶ repeat the error and name the type of error, for example, 'tense?' or 'word order?' or 'pronunciation?' (you can point to your mouth). In time, students will know this action indicates a pronunciation error (see Section 13 for guidance on correcting pronunciation);
▶ ask students to choose between a correct and incorrect version. For example, you might say, 'Is it "I go to the market yesterday" or "I went to the market yesterday"?';
▶ when a student cannot answer a question or cannot find a word, ask the class 'Can you help him (or her)?'.

Using your hands to indicate and correct errors (finger correction)

Hold your left hand up to the class with the palm facing you and your fingers spread out. Each finger represents the words of a sentence: your little finger is the first word. With your right hand, point to each finger as you say the word. Emphasize the incorrect word by moving the appropriate finger with your right hand.

Finger correction is mostly used for the following mistakes:

1. Incorrect word: for example, 'He live in my village'. Repeat the sentence, pointing to each finger for each word. When you reach the incorrect one, 'live', shake the finger with your right hand, repeating 'live' and say 'grammar' so that the student who made the mistake and the rest of the class have plenty of help in deciding what is the correct form, that is 'lives' (Figure 6.1).

2. Missing word: for example, 'My father is doctor'. Repeat the sentence, pointing to each finger for each word, and when you reach the missing word, indicate to students that there is a word missing. Encourage them to give you the missing word.

3. Missing contractions: for example, 'I will come with you'. Show all the words with your fingers and then squeeze the appropriate fingers together to show the contraction 'I'll come with you' (Figure 6.1).

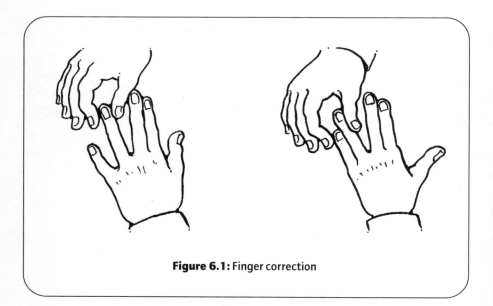

Figure 6.1: Finger correction

Correcting errors during the guided stage

At this stage, your students will probably be working in pairs or groups. The best way to correct errors is to walk round the class, monitoring and listening for errors. When you hear an error, quietly give the correct version and ask the students to repeat. Try not to disturb the practice too much.

If you cannot move round the desks or benches, you could encourage your students to work in threes instead of pairs and appoint a monitor (possibly a good student of English) to correct them. It may take time to establish a very supportive and co-operative atmosphere so that students accept that other students can correct them. Even if the monitor is not always correct, this technique often starts a discussion and keeps students involved in the learning process.

6.4 WAYS OF CORRECTING DURING THE PRODUCTION PHASE

During the Production phase, when your students are doing activities which are focused on fluency, monitor them and discreetly write down the errors you hear. After the activity, write some of the errors on the board (you need not say who made them) and ask the students to help you write the correct version. This is particularly useful when you hear several students making the same error. If you have the time and freedom to plan your own teaching programme, you can plan another lesson based on the errors which have occurred.

In a whole-class discussion, you can hand out cards with 'Error spotter' to a few students. These students note any errors they hear and report back at the end of the class (they do not need to say who made the mistakes). It is a good idea also to hand out a few 'Well done' cards to recognize particularly good phrases or vocabulary, or persistent errors which are now corrected. This is one way of keeping advanced students involved. Discuss the error spotters' notes at the end of the lesson.

7 / What Teaching Materials Can We Use?

7.1 OVERVIEW OF TEACHING AIDS

A speaking lesson can be very successful using nothing but the experience and imagination of the teacher and the students themselves. But there are many interesting and fun teaching aids which will improve the students' learning and motivation. Simple and realistic teaching aids help students understand and remember.

7.2 YOUR COURSE BOOK

The main resource that you are likely to have is your course book. Many teachers have to work with a set course book and a fixed and full syllabus, but there is scope to use or adapt the activities in this book and add them to your school's course book.

First, decide what the main learning points of each chapter are by looking at the teaching points. If the teaching points are not specified, look for yourself and decide what grammar, vocabulary, structures and functions are in each chapter. When you know the language content, you can decide exactly what to teach in your usual lesson, or in a PPP lesson.

Then you also need to think whether:

▶ there are different ways to teach the language in the chapter;
▶ there are different activities for the different parts of the chapter;
▶ there are enough suitable speaking activities;
▶ you can adapt or add suitable speaking activities.

For example, you could:

▶ use the reading text in a variety of ways (see Section 12);
▶ make the comprehension questions into pair or group work (see page 14);

Teaching aid	Example
Your course book	Texts, pictures, activities
The board	Texts, pictures, activities
Everyday objects that the teacher brings to the classroom	Fruit, toys, tools
Objects already in the classroom	Chairs, benches, desks, pupils, fan
Objects students bring to the classroom	A favourite or funny object or what each student has in his/her bag that day
Objects from outside the school	Stones, leaves, sticks, packaging
Puppets	For use with younger learners (see below)
Drawings, words or pictures stuck on large pieces of card (flashcards)	Pictures of food, clothing, sport, houses, people doing things
Drawings, words or pictures stuck on small cards	Pictures of objects (cut from catalogues or magazines), or drawings
Posters or big pictures	Any poster with pictures and writing, or special purpose teaching posters
Pictures in the English textbook	Copy and enlarge if you have this facility, or draw the picture larger
Large sheets of paper or a roll of paper	The teacher or students can make their own posters
Tape recorder	Professionally-made tapes and blank tapes for teachers or students to record material, or to listen to pre-recorded material
Radio	To listen to English-language programmes

And of course, our cheapest and most available teaching aids are the ideas, experience, imagination and beliefs of the students themselves.

Figure 7.1: Some examples of teaching aids

▶ adapt some of the grammar activities into practice or fluency activities (see pages 77–81);

▶ leave some of the grammar exercises for homework, as a reinforcement activity, and use the extra time in class for valuable speaking activities.

This way, you can use your existing materials and techniques and decide what you want to adapt and add.

7.3 USING THE BOARD

The board is the most useful teaching aid, and can provide a very good stimulus for speaking activities. It can be used to:

▶ give a visual context for presenting new language (for example, drawing pictures);

▶ provide pictures or charts as cues for different kinds of drills;

▶ record new vocabulary, pronunciation points, spellings or marking schemes for team activities;

▶ provide information in charts and diagrams as a basis for speaking activities;

▶ explain grammar points in a visual form;

▶ provide a source of text for students without books.

Divide the board into different areas for, say, new vocabulary, grammar, pictures, charts, text or exercises. Some information may be copied by students, some may remain for the whole lesson, and other areas may be cleaned for re-use during the lesson. A well-organized board is a great help to students, so try to plan what you will write or draw when you plan your lesson, and decide which parts of the board you will clean during the lesson. If you are not accustomed to drawing simple pictures quickly, it is a good idea to practise before the lesson. Don't forget that, for some activities, students can use the board too.

7.4 HOW TO MAKE TEACHING AIDS

Teaching aids need to be:

▶ large: if they are for the whole class to see, flashcards and posters must be really big. Pictures should be simple and letters clear and written with a dark pen;

▶ durable: if possible, laminate them or put them in a plastic protector;

► portable: remember you have to take your aids to school (possibly on your motorbike!);

► generic: so they can be used for different purposes. For instance, flash-cards or posters of food can be used to teach vocabulary (for example, names of different foods), for dialogues (for example, speaking about shopping) or for practising functional language (for example, questions and answers about favourite foods).

It is a lot of work to make a beautiful board game that you can only use once. So, if you make a board game, put numbers instead of instructions on the board. Players throw a dice or use a spinner (see page 86), move the correct number of spaces and then pick up a card with the number of the box on which they have landed. This card will have instructions, for example, 'Tell the group about your most exciting experience' or 'Name five articles of clothing'. This way, the game can be used many times because you only need to make more sets of cards for the different language your students need to practise.

Making and storing teaching aids

Teachers often complain that making teaching aids is very time consuming. Certainly, it does take a little time to think about effective teaching aids and then to make them. However, teaching aids are very effective in improving your students' learning, so this time is well spent.

Here are some tips:

► Store your teaching aids carefully in well-labelled boxes, plastic bags, folders or files. Concertina files are useful for storing pictures. Label the sections (see Figure 7.3, page 44).

► Remind students if you want them to bring any objects to the next lesson.

► Plan how you will use the board when you plan your lesson (see page 40).

► To make multiple copies of cards or strips for group work, do all your drawings or writing on one page, make the appropriate number of copies and cut and sort them afterwards.

► To make strong cards, cut up cardboard boxes and paste on pictures, or draw or write on the plain side.

► To reproduce pictures from your course book, practise simplifying the picture on scrap paper and then copy this onto a large sheet of paper.

► Packaging is a source of strong card, and can be used to present new language or in role play activities. You can help your students analyse and discuss any English words or phrases written on the package (for example, recommendations, advertising, advice to users).

▶ Find out about people who supply free posters and use the blank side for your own information. Cut cheap rolls of rough wrapping paper or wallpaper to the size you need.

▶ To make puppets, you can use a simple cut-out attached to a stick or cardboard cylinder, a sock, a plastic cup, a paper bag, a wooden spoon or your hand (see Figure 7.2).

You could get together with teachers from your school and other schools in your area and make teaching aids for your course book. Then you need to think about how the materials can be borrowed by teachers in other schools when they want them. Ideally, each school could produce a teacher's resource pack, but you will need to find a secure place to store the teaching aids. You will also need to decide how you can ensure things can be borrowed and returned in good condition (see Figure 7.3, page 44).

It does not always have to be the teachers who make teaching aids. You can involve students too. For example, students who finish their work early can copy drawings or make flash cards. Making the teaching aids can be a learning activity.

In this book, there are many examples of activities for each phase of a lesson. For each activity, we suggest suitable teaching aids and how you can best use them. Most teaching aids are simple and easy to make.

You will find more ideas on teaching aids and classroom resources in *The English Teacher's Handbook* (Baker and Westrup, VSO/Continuum) and in *How to Make Visual Aids* (Baird, VSO/Heinemann). Both these books are full of ideas for making low-cost resources from materials available in your environment.

In Sections 5–7, we looked at different aspects of managing your class and how to use teaching materials. In Sections 8–11, we look at ways of planning lessons which focus upon speaking. There are many activities which you can use or adapt with your students.

Figure 7.2: Some simple puppets

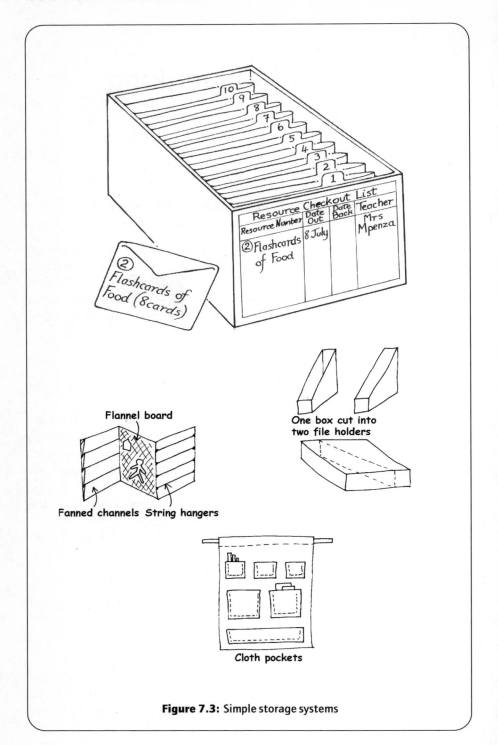

Figure 7.3: Simple storage systems

8 / Preparing for Speaking: Warmers

Warmers are short activities which teachers use at the beginning of a lesson. They are also sometimes called warm-up activities, starters or ice-breakers. Sometimes, they are related to the main objective of the lesson but they do not have to be. The purpose of warmers is to help students start to focus upon the lesson, to let them become accustomed to hearing and speaking English before the real lesson begins.

Warmers are useful for several reasons:

▶ the activities help students (and YOU) to get to know something about each other;
▶ they help students (and YOU) to learn each other's names. This is particularly helpful if you are starting to work with a new group of learners;
▶ they help to create a positive and relaxed atmosphere in the classroom;
▶ they can fill in the few minutes before the majority of the students arrive;
▶ they can help students revise what they have learnt in the past few lessons;
▶ they help to demonstrate that you expect students to participate actively in the lesson;
▶ they are fun!

So some warmers have a linguistic objective and some have a more social objective.

Organizing warmers

Most students enjoy doing warmers, so be careful that warmers don't take up most of the lesson (unless you planned it that way). Warmers should take less than five minutes in a thirty-minute lesson. They can be slightly longer if they are part of necessary revision of a previous lesson.

Most warmers need very little preparation but if they do, keep your ideas in a small notebook so you can use them again without further preparation. You can also add your own ideas and variations.

Remember that warmers are about communicating, so they should always be done in pairs, groups or teams. Divide the class into pairs or groups of four or five students. Demonstrate the activity first in front of the class, either doing it yourself with one student or with one pair or group. Then let the pairs or groups take part.

Some warmers can be done by two or three teams who come to the front of the class. Try to give as many students as possible the chance to take part in these public activities, so choose different students for each new activity. Remember to include some quiet students as well as those who enjoy performing in front of the class. It is very motivating for weaker students to be seen to succeed by the rest of the class.

Some students find a competitive element very motivating, so when you set up the groups or teams, give each a number, letter or name. You can give names from a lexical set (words about one lexical set/topic), like tigers, lions, monkeys and elephants (lexical set: animals), or different colours. Don't forget to keep the score. It is best to write it on the board. (See page 54 for some interesting ways of recording scores.) Don't forget to ask the class to clap the winning team.

8.2 SAMPLE WARMERS

We have grouped the sample warmers according to different classroom groups and contexts, but with a little imagination you can modify them to use in other ways. You can also make warmers easier or more difficult according to the vocabulary, grammar or topic you want your students to use. Remember to give clear, simple instructions and check that students understand what they have to do. When you set up an activity for the first time, you may need to do a brief practice.

Warmers for pairs

1. Favourites

Talk to your partner about your favourite food, sport or sportsperson, hobby, relative, friend or book and tell him/her why this is your favourite. Then listen to your partner telling you about his/her favourites and reasons why.

2. Me too!

Talk to your partner and try to find two things you have in common. Topics might be likes or dislikes, family relationships, things you own or things you do.

3. That's nice!

Tell your partner what you like about his/her appearance or character. Now listen to your partner saying what they like about you.

4. My life

Tell your partner what you did last night or last weekend and then listen to him/her telling you about what they did.

Warmers for pairs and small groups

5. Word collecting

Divide the class into groups. Give each group a topic and ask them to write down as many words on this topic as they can. The group with the longest list wins. You can then write the words on the board and check spelling and pronunciation. Each student should make a note of only two or three words which are new to them. You can also give different groups different topics but then be careful how you score. Some topics are more difficult than others!

Example topics: foods, weather, clothing, types of building, family members, geographical features (hills, mountains, rivers, cliffs, etc.), parts of the body, illnesses, wild or tame animals, types of books, types of TV programmes.

6. Definitions

Write about six definitions on the board (or dictate them). The groups work together to find words which match the definitions. You can use recently learned words.

Variation: you can also give words and ask for definitions (this is more difficult).

7. Same or different

Read out or write six words on the board. Groups/students then have to find words with similar meanings (synonyms) or opposite meanings (antonyms).

Examples: hot/warm (synonyms), long/short (antonyms).

8. Word groups

Write a collection of words in a random order all over the board and ask students to group them.

Example (vocabulary): butterfly, cup, bus, wasp, train, plate, bowl, bicycle, ant.

These can be grouped as:

▶ butterfly, wasp, ant (insects);
▶ bus, train, bicycle, (transport);
▶ cup, plate, bowl (crockery).

Variation (grammar): verbs which take a gerund, verbs which take an infinitive.

9. Scales

Draw a horizontal line on the board and write one word at each end to indicate a range, for example, cheap and expensive. This is a scale. Students have to fill in as many words as they can between the two given words, placing them in the correct order according to the meaning. You can then have a class discussion on whether the order is correct.

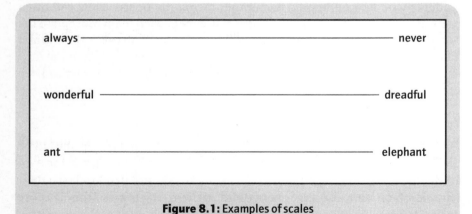

Figure 8.1: Examples of scales

10. Prefixes

Write a list of prefixes on the board. Give groups different prefixes. They have to find as many words as possible that can take this prefix.

Examples: un-, over-, under-, im-.

11.Word hunt

Write a long word on the board. Groups have to make as many short words as possible using only the letters in that word.

Example: EDUCATION (eat, ate, nut, cat, not, cut, date, etc.)

Warmers for teams

12.Team sentences

Select two teams, A and B, with up to ten students in each team, and get them to face each other. The first person in team A says one word to start a sentence. Then the first person in team B says a word to continue this sentence. The second person in team A adds a word to continue the sentence. The teams alternate and continue adding words. The sentence must make sense and it must be grammatically correct. The aim is to make the sentence as long as possible. The team which finishes the sentence is the loser.

13.Touch the box

Draw six boxes on the board, with big spaces between them. In each box, write one new word that students have recently learned. These words can either be in English or in the students' first language. Select two teams of six students who line up behind each other facing the board. Now call out a translation of one of the words. The first student in each team must go to the board and touch the appropriate word. The first one to do this is the winner. The next two students in the line have their turn when you read out the next word, and so on until all the words have been tested. Don't forget to keep score.

14. Guess the word

Divide the class into a maximum of four groups. The first group should be the front left of the classroom, the second group the front right, and so on across the classroom (see Figure 8.2). Students do not need to leave their seats. Each group must send one representative to the front of the class. He or she stands facing the group with their back to the board so what is written on the board cannot be seen. Now you write a word on the board which students have recently learned (or need to revise). Students in the groups can see this and have to call out definitions to their representative who cannot see the word and has to try to guess it. Of course, the students must not use the word on the board in their definition.

Figure 8.2: Students playing 'Guess the word'

Round-the-class warmers

In a small class, round-the-class warmers work best if students can sit in a circle. In a bigger class, you can try to make several circles. But if students cannot move out of their seats, simply nominate students at random, so that the 'circle' has members all around the classroom.

15. Learning names

Each student thinks of something they like which begins with the same letter as their name. Then one student starts the activity. She says: 'My name is Leila and I like lemons'. Then the next student (either in the circle or anywhere in the classroom) says, 'My name is Ismail and I like ice cream and her name is Leila and she likes lemons.' The third student continues, 'My name is Fatima and I like fishing and his name is Ismail and he likes ice cream and her name is Leila and she likes lemons'.

You can do this activity with up to about sixteen students, but of course it becomes more difficult for students towards the end of the activity.

Variation: to make it easier, or for younger students, you could limit each student to remembering only two or three people and the things they like.

16. I went to market

Each student has to think of something he or she can buy at the market. Then the first student starts and says, for example, 'I went to market and I bought some eggs'. The second student then says, 'I went to market and I bought some eggs and some bread'. The third then says, 'I went to market and I bought some eggs, some bread and some tomatoes', and so on.

17. Alphabet chains

The first student says, for example, 'My father is an actor'. The next student says, 'My mother is a baker'. Student three says, 'My uncle is a carpenter', and so on through the alphabet.

Variation: you can leave out difficult letters.

You can ask students to suggest other topics for this alphabet chain (fruit, names, food and so on).

Warmers using the blackboard or posters

18. Crosswords

Make a very simple crossword using words that students have recently learnt. You can draw this on the board, on a poster you have made or give students copies, one for each pair or group. Either give students copies of the clues, dictate them or read them out.

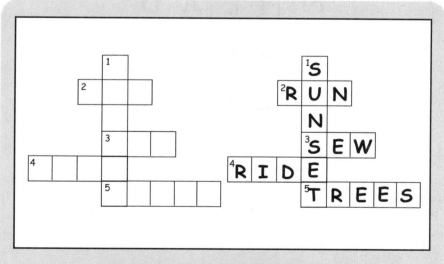

Figure 8.3: An example of a crossword

Variation: when students can do this well, give each group about six words they have recently learnt and ask them to make the crossword and clues. They can then pass these to another group to discuss and complete. You may have to check that the clues are good before they are passed to another group.

19. Word search

Make a word search on a poster and stick this on the board for all students to see. In groups, students have to spot the new vocabulary hidden in the puzzle.

Figure 8.4: A word search

20. Mystery boxes

Draw about six boxes on the board and put one word inside each. These words are clues to some information about you, for example, *Liverpool, 37, Bruno, 2001, 11.*

Students have to ask you questions to find out what this information about you means.

Answers to the example:

▶ *Liverpool* is my football team.
▶ I live at *37* Oxford Street.
▶ My dog is called *Bruno*.
▶ I trained to be a teacher in *2001*.
▶ I have *11* cousins.

Students can now make their own boxes (maybe only three for younger students) and repeat the activity in pairs or groups.

This warmer is more suitable for advanced students who know a range of question types, such as, 'Were you born in 1968?', 'Do you come from Liverpool?', 'Are you 37 years old?', 'Is your husband called Bruno?'.

Moving around the classroom

Here are three warmers which are fun and which help students to relax and get to know each other. They are best suited to small classes (or teachers' workshops) where there is room to move around.

21. Topic circle

Divide the students in two groups and get them to stand in two circles: an inner circle and an outer circle. The students in the outside circle face a partner in the inside circle. Call out a topic and ask students to speak with their partner on this topic in English for two minutes. After this time, call for silence. The people in the outer circle now move clockwise by three or four people, so that they have a new partner. Now give a new topic and repeat the time limit. Continue for three or four more topics.

Ideas for topics:

▶ What is your name, what does it mean and why were you given it?
▶ What is your favourite food? When do you eat it? How do you prepare it?

22. Alphabet circle

Ask students to stand in a circle. They must be in alphabetical order according to their first name round the circle. Now each must say their name and one piece of information about themselves.

Variation: as a group, the class can try to remember names and information about class members. The teacher can prompt them, for example, 'Who likes to play basketball?', and the class replies, 'Estrella does'.

23. Mystery lines

Divide students into two groups, no more than fifteen in each group. Whisper to each group a reason for standing in a line in a particular order. They have to discuss this secretly and then stand in line in the correct order facing the other line. Each person has a partner in the other line. Now, opposite pairs have to find out the reason why the line is arranged in this order, asking questions that only require a 'yes/no' answer.

Ideas for topics:

► your shoe size;
► birth dates;
► how long it takes you to travel to college/work.

Scoring competitive games

24. Shark attack

On the board, draw two sets of steps leading to the sea. These represent two teams. Draw or make a cut-out of a person at the top of each flight of steps. Ask questions. For each incorrect answer, the person moves down one step until he/she falls into the water and is carried off by the shark!

Variation: a more positive version, perhaps more suitable for younger learners, is to have steps to go up for each correct answer to collect a 'treasure' at the top.

25. Noughts and crosses

Make a matrix on the board (see Figure 8.5). One team places a nought in a box for each correct answer they give, the other team places a cross. The team with three of their own symbols in a row is the winner.

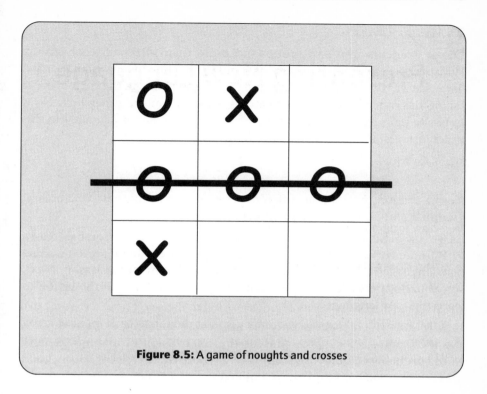

Figure 8.5: A game of noughts and crosses

9 / Presenting New Language

In this section, we look at different ways of presenting new vocabulary, grammar and functional language using speaking.

As we saw in Section 4, speaking is an important part of a lesson based on a PPP framework. In this kind of lesson, the teacher usually presents some new language at the beginning or near the beginning of the lesson. Next, students do speaking activities during the Practice phase of the lesson to learn this new language.

In a lesson which focuses only on improving speaking skills without a specific language focus, the presentation or revision of a language item would probably be quite brief. However, in both these types of lesson, good presentation will help students to understand, remember and be able to use new language.

9.1 THE PRESENTATION PHASE OF A PPP LESSON ON SPEAKING

The Presentation phase of a language lesson based on a PPP framework is similar in some ways to traditional language teaching. In both teaching approaches, the teacher presents the students with new information. She or he is at the front of the class, next to the board, and talks to the whole class.

Here are some important features of the Presentation phase of a PPP lesson:

- ▶ This phase should only last about five to ten minutes. The rest of the lesson should be used for practice, or practice and production.
- ▶ The information the teacher gives is for students to use later in the lesson. It should not just be written down and memorized.
- ▶ Teachers should try to involve students in this stage as much as possible (see elicitation, page 58).

When presenting language it is important to include four things:

► what the new language means;
► when the new language is normally used;
► the grammatical form;
► the pronunciation of the new language, that is, the sounds and stress and the intonation pattern.

9.2 PRESENTING MEANING, USE, FORM AND PRONUNCIATION

To help students understand the meaning of the new language and when it is used, you must put the language into a clear context. There are many effective ways of doing this:

► The students read a text or listen to a tape which contains examples of the new language. This can be a story or a dialogue, spoken by the teacher or by puppets.
► You can use real objects or pictures, or draw objects, people or a situation on the board.
► You can tell the students about a situation which demonstrates the meaning of the new language.
► You can mime (act without speaking) an action or emotion or act out a role play or dialogue which helps show what the new language is, what it means and when it is used.

Showing the pronunciation of a new language item

You can demonstrate difficult sounds by showing where in the mouth the sound is made, how the lips should be shaped, the place of the tongue, and so on. You can also do this by using the hands as a model of the mouth or by doing a quick drawing of the mouth on the board.

Word stress can be shown by writing the word and marking stress in the traditional way as shown in dictionaries (for example, ed u ca' tion), or by drawing a big circle over the stressed syllable and small circles for the unstressed syllables. You can also show where the stress is by punching the air when you say the stressed part of a word or the stressed word of a sentence.

Intonation can be shown by drawing the up and down pattern of a phrase in the air with the hand (see Section 13 for more information on pronunciation).

9.3 STAGES OF THE PRESENTATION PHASE

To make sure that you cover all the important information about a new language item in the Presentation phase, it is best to go through the following steps:

▶ Set the scene. You can try to elicit the new language from your students. See elicitation below.
▶ Model the new language, saying it two or three times, demonstrating the stress or intonation patterns.
▶ Ask students to repeat the new language several times out loud, first the whole class, then in groups, then in pairs.
▶ Use questions to check that students understand the meaning of the new words, structure or functional language.
▶ Write the new language on the board, checking the stress and the spelling with the students.
▶ If necessary, explain the grammar of the new language using the board.
▶ Ask students to copy the information from the board into their notebooks.

Elicitation

The Presentation phase is naturally quite teacher-centred. However, it is still useful to involve students to help them become more responsible for their own learning and to encourage them to use as much English as they can. Elicitation is a useful way to involve students, and it will also help you, the teacher, to find out how much your students know, or how much they have remembered from previous lessons. Eliciting is a form of questioning. Elicitation can be very specific, for example, trying to encourage students to say the word or phrase that you intend to teach. It can also be very open, for example, collecting students' ideas or opinions about a picture, some sentences or a topic.

Of course, if your students never hear English outside the classroom or if they have not yet learned certain words or phrases, you will be able to do less elicitation. However, it is often possible to build upon language they already know. Sometimes your students will be glad to have the opportunity to show their knowledge and will surprise you by how much they know! A golden rule is that the teacher never tells the students something they already know or can guess.

Here are some examples of how to use elicitation.

1. Eliciting new vocabulary

Teacher:	(showing the class a mango) 'What is this?'
Students:	'A fruit.'
Teacher:	'That's right, it's a fruit. Listen: It's a mango.'
Students:	'It's a mango.'

2. Eliciting a new grammatical structure

Present continuous

Teacher:	(showing the class a picture of a man running) 'Tell me about this man.'
Students:	'He runs.'
Teacher:	'Nearly. Listen: he is running.'
Students:	'He is running.'

Question formation

Teacher:	(writing 'Peter can play the guitar' on the board) 'How do we make a question?'
Student(s)	'You must put a question mark after "guitar".'
Teacher:	'That's right. You must put a question mark after "guitar", and you must move "can" in front of "Peter". Well done.'

3. Eliciting functional language

Making a request

Teacher:	(miming that she is very hot and looking at the fan – make sure it is switched off!) 'I'm very hot. The fan is not on. You are near the switch. What do I say?'
Student(s)	'Switch fan on, please.'
Teacher:	'Good, nearly right. Listen: Would you switch the fan on, please?'
Students:	'Would you switch the fan on, please?'

4. Eliciting ideas from a picture

Practising vocabulary

Teacher:	(showing a picture of two people. One is boarding a train) 'Who do you think these people are?'
Student A:	'Husband and wife.'

Student B:	'Brother and sister.'
Teacher:	'Where do you think the man is going?'
Student C:	'To the city.'
Teacher:	'He has a very smart suit on. Why do you think he's going to the city?'

and so on.

9.4 PRESENTING VOCABULARY

Students can learn up to six new words effectively in one lesson. Remember that vocabulary includes not only single words but also compound words, phrases, collocations (words which naturally go together, like 'absolutely exhausted') and idiomatic phrases and idioms.

Examples: cotton wool, black and white, to hold your tongue, to be over the moon.

Some quick and effective ways of presenting vocabulary are:

▶ mime (acting without words): particularly useful for actions, adverbs, emotions;
▶ pictures: build up a collection of pictures from magazines or pictures you have drawn. Practise drawing simple pictures on the board;
▶ realia (real objects): bring objects from outside the classroom or use objects in the classroom;
▶ synonyms or antonyms: ask 'What is another word for . . . ?', or 'What is the opposite of . . . ?'.

Situations: tell the students a few sentences which describe the word (without using it).

Example: 'I worked till 10 o'clock every night last week. I feel very tired. I have no energy. I want to sleep. I am absolutely . . . ' (*answer*: exhausted).

Do not be afraid to give a direct translation for difficult abstract words, like 'justice' or 'although'. This is often much quicker and easier for the students than other techniques.

9.5 PRESENTING GRAMMAR

There are many ways of presenting grammar to students and you probably already know and use different methods. The approach you use depends on your students, your textbook, the style of teaching you and your students are most comfortable with and the grammatical structure you are teaching. But remember that it is still very important to make sure students understand the meaning, use and pronunciation of the new language. You also need to show the students how to form the grammatical structure at some stage in the lesson.

Presenting language directly

Direct (or overt) presentation of grammar is when the teacher explains the grammatical rules and other information. This is often done in the students' first language. To teach this way, you must make sure that students understand grammatical names like parts of speech (nouns, verbs, adjectives etc.) and grammatical function (subject, verb, object, conjunction and so on).

For example, to teach the negative, the teacher first writes a positive sentence on the board: 'Ester likes football'. Underneath, he writes: 'Kennedy DOES NOT like football'. He then tells the students that to make a negative sentence in the third person singular, you must put the subject, then 'does not' before the main verb. 'Does' is a modal auxiliary, 'not' indicates the negative and these are followed by the infinitive of 'like' without 'to', followed by the object, 'football'. Sometimes it is useful to label the parts of speech on the board or write a formula, for example:

| Kennedy | does | not | | like | | football. |

Subject + auxiliary verb + 'not' + infinitive (without 'to') + object.

Presenting grammar through a text

After you have introduced a new grammatical structure, students can practise it by reading and finding the structure within a text. They can underline each instance of it or list them in their notebooks. They then have to work out the grammatical rule or formula. They can do this through discussion in pairs or groups.

Presenting grammar through comparison

Structure: 'Enough' can be an adjective which goes in front of a noun; 'enough' can also be an adverb which follows an adjective or verb.

Write two similar grammatical structures on the board. Students have to discuss in pairs or groups what the difference is and compare the meaning and use of the phrases. For example:

A: We don't have enough books for everyone.

B: The bookshelf is not big enough for all those books.

Presenting language indirectly

Indirect (or covert) teaching of grammar is when the teacher does not start with an explanation of the grammar but helps students to understand the information they need to know using other methods. This can be helpful if students are not familiar or comfortable with the grammatical terms used in overt teaching (see page 61).

In this approach, you do not draw the students' attention to any specific grammatical information but use situations, pictures or the students' own knowledge to present the meaning, use and pronunciation. You can then teach the form of the structure.

Presenting through situations

Grammar and use: present continuous tense ('are living') used for temporary situations.

Tell a simple story or anecdote or draw a series of pictures which demonstrates the use and meaning of the structure.

Example: you say, 'Our house was flooded last week, so we are living with my grandparents. We hope to go back to our own house next week.'

Presenting through pictures and real objects

Grammar and use: we use 'in' for something that is inside something else.

Draw on the board, show a large picture or take a classroom object with something inside it.

Example: place the board cleaner in a box and say, 'The cleaner is in the box.'

Presenting through students' own knowledge

The teacher elicits some information that the students know. This can be done in the students' first language.

Grammar and use: comparative used to compare sizes.

Teacher:	'Tell me something about Hanoi.'
Student A:	'It is a big city.'
Teacher:	'That's right. Now tell me something about Danang.'
Student B:	'Danang is a small city.'
Teacher:	'So what can we say, in English, about these two cities?'
Student C:	'Hanoi is big. Danang is small.'

Teacher: 'Excellent. Listen: Hanoi is BIGGER THAN Danang. And Danang is . . . ?'

Student D: 'Danang is smaller than Hanoi.'

9.6 PRESENTING FUNCTIONAL LANGUAGE

When working with students on new functional language, it is not always necessary to start by explaining the grammatical structure. Students first need to understand the whole phrase, when it is used and in what context. The context will tell us how formal or informal we can be, because each function has many exponents and students need to know which they should use.

▶ To a friend, we say, 'Fancy a drink?'
▶ To our boss, we say, 'Would you like something to drink?'
▶ If we are speaking to the prime minister, we would say, 'May I offer you something to drink, madam?'

The most useful phrase is a neutral level of formality, which means it can be used in many situations. In this example, the second phrase is the neutral one. Less advanced students only need to learn the neutral phrase at first. They can learn others as they became more fluent.

It is important to make students aware that there are several levels of formality and that there are many ways of expressing that formality.

Presenting functions through mime, acting or puppets

For younger learners, you can use one puppet in each hand and let them speak to each other. (See Figure 9.1.)

Mime that you have forgotten your pen. Look in your pocket and bag. You can then act both speakers in this dialogue:

Teacher (as Teacher A) says, 'Could you lend me a pen?'

Teacher (as Teacher B) says, 'Yes, of course.' (Mimes giving a pen to Teacher A.) 'Here you are.'

You can also do a presentation that involves the students. Once again, perform a mime. This time, you have forgotten your book. Look around for a student who has a book.

Figure 9.1: Teacher using puppets

Teacher:	'I have forgotten my book. I need to read to you. Joseph has a book. What do I say to him?'
Student A:	'May I borrow your book?'
Teacher:	'Good. Joseph, may I borrow your book?'
Joseph:	(giving you his book) 'Yes, of course. Here you are.'

It is a good idea to present several similar situations which use the same exponent, so that students are completely clear what phrase to use. For example:

Teacher:	'I don't know how to spell "castle". May I borrow your dictionary?'
Student A:	'Yes, of course. Here you are.'

Presenting functional language with different levels of formality through reading

Write several sentences for one function on the board. There should be a variety of levels of formality, for example:

- Can I borrow your pen?
- Would you mind if I borrow that book?
- Can I possibly borrow that book?
- Can I borrow some money for the bus?
- Would it be possible to borrow your motorbike tomorrow?
- I wonder if it would be possible to borrow some money for a couple of months?

On the other side of the board, write the words: your boss (or your head teacher), your teacher, your sister, the manager of a bank, another student.

Now students can discuss which phrase you can use with which person. (Note: longer phrases are often used when there is a greater social difference between the two speakers, or when the task is more difficult to do!) At a lower level, only discuss two or three phrases. Then discuss the results with the whole class. (See page 88 for practice activities to follow this kind of presentation.)

Presenting functional language through listening

Choose a student who speaks English well and read a short dialogue with them which contains several functional exponents in front of the class. Ask half the class to listen and write down phrases which are used to make suggestions to people. Ask the other half of the class to listen and write down phrases which are used to express uncertainty.

Example

Student A:	'Why don't you stop studying and go to work in the Sunset Hotel?'
Student B:	'I might, but I really want to pass my exam.'
Student A:	'You could always study in the evening.'
Student B:	'I suppose so, but I need help from my teacher.'
Student A:	'Why not ask your friends to help you?'
Student B:	'Well, I'll see. I can't make up my mind because I need to earn some money to pay for my school books.'
Student A:	'Perhaps you could go and see my uncle. He is the cook at the hotel. I think he can help you.'
Student B:	'I can't decide. Maybe I'll go and see him after my exam.'

Check and discuss the phrases with the class. Each student should record a couple of phrases for making suggestions and expressing uncertainty.

Remember that students must understand functional language and how it changes according to the speaker before they start practising the language.

In the next section, we look at the different ways students can practise new language.

10 / Practising Speaking

In this section, we include ways of practising speaking skills and of using speaking to practise new vocabulary and grammar and functional language. (For information on functional language, see Section 9.) Students need a lot of practice in using the new language they have learnt in the Presentation phase. The Practice phase is the main part of the lesson, which can also include practice in listening, reading and writing. It is important that, before the Practice phase begins, students understand the meaning of the words and phrases they use, so you must make sure of this during the Presentation phase.

Students may be very shy about speaking English for many different reasons. Choral drilling can help by giving them the chance to practise making sounds, words and phrases without having to say anything alone in front of the whole class. Working in pairs and groups is another way of giving students time to practise in a supportive atmosphere.

The activities in this section are examples from which you can select those which are useful for your course and meet your students' needs.

Stages of the Practice phase

During the Practice phase of a lesson, you will work with your students to practise speaking in different ways at different stages:

▶ controlled practice stage;
▶ guided or less controlled practice stage.

At the beginning of the Practice phase, the teacher controls everything students say and corrects the pronunciation, sentence construction and use of the language. We call this the controlled practice stage. There are many ways this kind of speaking practice can be done so that students learn to be accurate.

Later in the Practice phase, students do activities with less help and control from you. This is the guided or less controlled practice stage. Students practise the language in pairs or groups, but now you only guide the activity. You still monitor the work, walking quietly around the pairs or groups, listening, sometimes correcting and making sure students know what they have to do.

At the end of the Practice phase, students should be able to use the new language reasonably well, and to speak more fluently using the language they have learnt.

10.2 CONTROLLED PRACTICE STAGE: GRAMMAR AND VOCABULARY

Students can practise speaking:

► individually by responding to the teacher;
► by speaking together in pairs or groups. The best size for group work is four or five, so that each student has a chance to speak;
► in chorus, so the whole class practises by speaking together at the same time;
► in two big groups who can then practise a dialogue, each half of the class speaking in unison and taking one part of the dialogue;
► in rows or smaller groups.

We call these last three ways of drilling choral drilling (see page 32 for ways of organizing pair and group work).

During the Presentation phase, the students hear the new language several times. During the controlled practice stage of the Practice phase, students learn the language in its context.

When you start drilling, isolate the new language and say it several times so that students can hear it and repeat it accurately. When leading choral drilling, make sure that:

► you use very simple instructions, like 'repeat', 'all together', 'again';
► all students speak together;
► they speak at a normal speed;
► they all imitate not only the individual sounds but also the stresses and intonation pattern;
► they speak naturally and with energy.

Raise both hands and conduct the class, so that students know exactly when to start speaking together. If you have divided the class into groups, indicate clearly which group should be speaking.

Although drilling is an extremely useful way of practising, it can also become mechanical. Here are five ways to make it more interesting and realistic:

i) Instead of drilling only the word or phrase which your students need to practise, use drills which require a response, in other words make them more similar to a real conversation.

Drills can be in the form of question and answer:

- ▶ 'How did you come to school today?'
- ▶ 'I came by bus.'
- ▶ 'How did you come to school today?'
- ▶ 'I came by bicycle.'

or of statement and response:

- ▶ 'I really like your new hairstyle.'
- ▶ 'Oh, thanks.'
- ▶ 'I really like your new dress.'
- ▶ 'Oh, thanks.'

ii) You can use different cues to which students respond. These cues can be an object, a word written on a card or on the board, a picture on a card, a drawing on the board or a word spoken by the teacher. However, pictures and real objects are more memorable and encourage students to think about what they are saying and not just repeat what they hear. You could also hold up a card with a happy face for yes and a sad face for no. In this way, students also learn to apply an English word directly to the object or situation, which is better than learning through a continual process of translation.

Some teachers put cards with pictures of two people on either side of the board and point to them as each says their part of the drill. It is a good idea to give characters names. Puppets also work well. (Figure 10.1.)

iii) You can vary the people who take part in the practice. We call this changing the classroom interaction pattern.

iv) You can give students some choice in how they respond. In classes where students have a wider vocabulary, you can make drills more realistic by letting students add their own ideas to personalize the drill.

Another kind of activity (see p. 72), where one student has to find out some information that he or she does not know from another student, is called an information gap activity.

Figure 10.1: Cue cards with happy and sad faces

v) Longer drills are sometimes difficult for students. To help them, begin by making them repeat the last few words of the phrase. When they can repeat these accurately, add drill words that come before these in the sentence. Keep adding the words before until you can drill from the beginning of the sentence. Be careful to maintain the correct intonation pattern. This kind of drill is called back chaining.

Example:

Teacher:	. . . in the garden.
Students:	in the garden.
Teacher:	. . . working in the garden.
Students:	working in the garden.
Teacher:	. . . my weekends working in the garden.
Students:	my weekends working in the garden.
Teacher:	I spend my weekends working in the garden.
Students:	I spend my weekends working in the garden.

When practising new vocabulary, students should be very familiar with the grammar used to practise the new words. Likewise, when practising a grammatical structure which is new to them, students should be familiar with the vocabulary used.

Activities for the controlled practice stage

Here are some examples of drills, which you can use to practise any new language.

26. Repetition drills

In repetition drills, students repeat the language you have presented as accurately as possible.

Materials: words or pictures on the board, or flash cards with words or pictures.

As you repeat the words to be practised, indicate the appropriate word or picture on the board or flash card. Students need to hear and repeat new language four or five times. Don't forget the importance of correct intonation and both word and sentence stress (see Section 13, page 130). Here is one way of doing a repetition drill.

Example:

Teacher: 'This is my bag. Repeat.'

Students: 'This is my bag.'

Teacher: 'This is my bag. Again.'

Students: 'This is my bag.'

Variation 1: it is fun to ask students to work in groups and to put an object of their own in the centre of the group. They can then practise structures such as, 'This is my bag', 'This is my comb', 'This is my book', 'This is my ruler' and so on. They can then move on to more complex grammatical structures like, 'That is her ruler', 'That is his book'.

Other language that can be practised in this way is 'May I have' or 'May I borrow', for example, 'May I borrow your ruler?', 'Yes, of course'.

Variation 2: another way of organizing repetition drills is for students to speak in turn around the whole class or a group. In a large class, you may not have time to go around the whole class and this could be boring, so nominate students to participate in the drill from any part of the classroom.

It is important to do repetition drills for new vocabulary, even with advanced students. More abstract words, for example, justice, thorough, subsidiary, cannot usually be cued through pictures. You can cue them by simply saying the word or showing it written on a flash card.

27. Substitution drills (Figure 10.2)

Substitution drills are similar to repetition drills, but they give students more choice in building correct sentences, phrases or dialogues.

Materials: the board or flash cards with words or pictures.

At first, ask students to repeat exactly what you say, prompted by a word or picture cue. Now change one word or phrase in the sentence, showing the appropriate flash card or point to the word or picture on the board. Students repeat again, using the newly cued word or words.

Example:

Teacher: (Showing picture of a mango.) 'Do you like mangoes? Repeat.'

Students: 'Do you like mangoes?' (Drill this several times.)

Teacher: (Showing picture of a pineapple.) 'Do you like pineapples? Repeat.' (Drill this several times.)

Teacher: 'Yes, I do. Repeat.'

Students: 'Yes, I do.' (Drill this several times.)

Teacher: 'No, I don't. Repeat.'

Students: 'No, I don't.' (Drill this several times.)

You now also have the basis of a good question-and-answer drill.

Variation: charts are an easy way to help students practise substitution drills. You can quickly draw them on the board (see Figure 10.2, page 73, for a simple like and dislike chart). This gives maximum help to the students while allowing them some word choice. This kind of drill can easily be followed by a communicative or personalized drill, where students ask each other about their own likes and dislikes.

28. Information gap drills

Materials: paper, cards or students' notebooks.

If you have enough resources to make cards, ask students to help you make them. They must draw carefully and precisely. In a small class, you can make the cards yourself, one for each student, and make matching pairs. Students can walk around the class, trying to find out who has the card which matches theirs. Collect the cards at the end of the drill. You can use them with another class or lend them to another teacher.

Draw a simple house on the board. It has a door and four windows. Now draw another house on the board with three windows and two doors.

Does	he she Peter Iman	like	oranges? bananas? peaches? milk? fish?

Do Does	you they she he Shiv Alia	like	oranges? bananas? peaches? milk? fish?

Figure 10.2: Substitution drills

Now ask a student who speaks English confidently to come to the front of the class. You and the student now stand with your backs to each other, each of you looking at a different house. Now practise the information gap drill:

Teacher: 'Does your house have three windows?'

Student: 'Yes, it has. Does your house have three windows?'

Teacher: 'No, it hasn't. It has four windows.'

Student: 'Does your house have two doors?'

Teacher: 'No, it hasn't. It has one door. Does your house have two doors?'

Student: 'Yes, it has.'

Variation 1: this very simple drill can be changed to practise different vocabulary. For example, houses can be of two different colours ('Do you have a red house?') or you can add a simple tree on the left or right ('Do you have a tree on the right of your house?').

Variation 2: in large classes with few resources, make two posters with different information and put one at each end of the classroom so students can read them. Divide the students into pairs. Ask one student of each pair to read the poster at the back of the class and to create a conversation with their partner. Possible topics might be:

Poster 1: Items of food with prices;

Poster 2: A shopping list with different items.

Now students can practise language like:

'Do you have any . . . ?'

Answer: 'Yes, I do', or 'No, I don't'.

'How much do . . . cost?'

Answer: '3,000 kwachas a kilo'.

Then students can make their own lists and practise in pairs.

29. Questionnaires

Once students can do questions and answers in drills, they can compile a class or group questionnaire from their answers. Using questionnaires can either be a very controlled language practice activity, or it can be a guided or fluency activity. Questionnaires in the style of a gap-fill exercise make students work harder (see Figure 10.3).

Class 4: Gap-fill questionnaire		
	Yes	No
1. Can you _____ a bicycle?		
2. _____ _____ dance?		
3. Can you _____ a musical instrument?		
4. Can you _____ a cake?		
5. Can you _____ a picture?		

Figure 10.3: Gap-fill questionnaire

Class 4: Questionnaire

	Grace	Mpenza	Emmanuel	Merciline
1. What time do you get up?				
2. When do you eat lunch?				
3. When do you go home?				
4. What time do you eat your dinner?				

Figure 10.4: Questionnaire

Materials: paper or students' notebooks. Draw a matrix for the questions and answers on the board and let students copy this into their notebooks.

Possible topics:

▶ How do you come to school?
▶ Where have you been?/What transport have you travelled in?
▶ What time do you get up/have lunch/go to bed?
▶ What is your favourite TV/radio programme, book, magazine?

You can ask students to write up the results of their questionnaires as a writing activity.

Variation: with more advanced students, you can ask questions about more sophisticated topics, depending on your context and the students' interests. You can build up a profile of the interests and opinions of all the members of the class.

30. Disappearing dialogues

Materials: the board or a large sheet of paper (the back of a poster).

Read a short dialogue a few times. You can read out both parts and, if you wish, use two puppets. Elicit the dialogue from your students line by line and write it on the board or on a poster. Now do a drill, with groups taking one half of the dialogue each. Next students can practise in pairs. While they do pair practice, erase (or stick small squares of paper to the poster to cover) certain words or phrases. Students should continue to 'read' the dialogues, remembering and saying the words that are missing. Now erase more words from the dialogue. Continue until the whole dialogue has been erased. Students now have to remember the whole dialogue. Finish by asking pairs to volunteer to perform the dialogue for the class.

You can introduce some variety into this activity by asking students to work in pairs and to write out the dialogue when there are very few words left on the board or when the whole dialogue has been rubbed out.

31. Kim's game

Materials: a selection of real objects or pictures of objects (about fifteen objects) cut out from magazines or newspapers, and stuck on a large sheet of paper. Alternatively, you can draw the objects on a large sheet of paper.

Students must know what these objects are called in English. It is best if some of them are things they have learnt over the past few weeks.

In a small class, place the objects on a table and let students look at them for one minute. Then cover the objects with a large cloth. If you use a picture hold it up in front of the class, then remove it after one minute. Now, working in pairs or groups, students try to remember what the objects were. Then, you can elicit them.

Student A: 'There were some nails.'

Student B: 'There was a pair of scissors.'

Student C: 'There were some sweets.'

This very simple activity is useful for learning related vocabulary, such as technical names for tools, geometrical shapes or colours.

32. Guessing games

Materials: none.

There are many guessing games which can be used either for controlled drills or advanced fluency activities. For example, you think of a colour without telling the students. They have to find out what colour you are thinking of by asking you questions:

Student 1:   'Is is red?'

Teacher: 'No, it isn't.'

Student 2:   'Is it yellow?'

Teacher: 'No, it isn't.'

Student 3:   'Is it green?'

Teacher: 'Yes, it is.'

Now play this in groups, with students taking turns to answer the questions.

Variation 1: think of an object in the classroom. Students ask questions using more difficult language, such as 'Is it round?', 'Is it flat?', 'Is it made of . . . ?', 'Is it used for . . . ?'.

Variation 2: you can practise prepositions by pretending you have hidden an object. Students ask questions using language such as 'Is it near the door?', 'Is it on the teacher's desk?'. Another way of practising prepositions of place is to pretend that you are hiding in a place that everyone knows, but don't tell the students. They can use any questions to find out where you are.

Variation 3: think of a famous person whom everyone has heard of. For a less controlled drill, students can now ask questions to find out who you are thinking of, using any language and questions they know: 'Are you alive?', 'Are you a woman?', 'Are you famous?', and so on. (When you limit the number of questions to twenty, this activity is usually called twenty questions.)

10.3 LESS CONTROLLED AND GUIDED PRACTICE STAGES: GRAMMAR AND VOCABULARY

Activities for the less controlled and guided Practice stage

33. Practising use of tenses

Materials: the board or small cards.

Write a list of key time words or phrases on the board or make sets of cards for each group with one key word or phrase on each card. Key time phrases are those which indicate which form of a verb should be used, for example:

always, never, often, just . . . when . . . , at the moment, and so on.

Allocate a few key words or phrases to each group and decide on one verb that everyone must use, for example, 'drive' or 'eat'. Check that students know the form of the verbs that you expect them to use (eat, am/is eating, ate, have/had eaten, and so on). Groups have to make a correct sentence which uses their key word or phrase and a correct form of the chosen verb.

Examples:

▶ I ALWAYS eat supper at six o'clock.
▶ I have NEVER eaten blackberries.
▶ I OFTEN ate with my friends when I was at college.
▶ I had JUST eaten my supper when my friend arrived.

34. Filling in forms

Materials: the board.

Draw a form on the board which has to be filled in with different information. Ask students to copy this form into their notebooks. Demonstrate the activity with a student who speaks English well and then let students work in pairs. Give the students time to read the form and to decide on answers (they may have to invent some information about themselves) before starting the activity. Do the activity twice, to let students play both roles. Then ask a few pairs to demonstrate their conversation in front of the class.

Possible topics are any situation which requires a form to be filled in, for example, an application for a student visa, an application to attend a course, an application to register for a new school and so on.

Example: arriving at a hotel. One student is the guest and the other is the receptionist. (This example may be more suitable for adult learners.)

Hotel registration form

Name:

Age:

Nationality:

Date of birth:

Address:

Profession:

Travelling from:

Travelling to:

---

35. Information gap diaries

Materials: students' notebooks.

Ask students to work in pairs. One of each pair is an 'A' student, and the other is a 'B' student. All students make a diary with space for seven days of the week. All 'A' students write down events they are going to do (real or imaginary) in four of the days (for example, Monday, Tuesday, Thursday and Friday). All 'B' students write down events for the other three days. Tell everyone which days are 'A' students' days, and which are 'B' students' days. Now students work in pairs. The 'A' students ask questions to find out the events for the 'B' days and write the answers in their diary. The 'B' students answer, then ask questions about the missing events for the 'A' days, and write the answers in their diary.

	Student A	Student B
Monday	Play football	?
Tuesday	Meet Grace and Mpenza	?
Wednesday	?	Swim in the river
Thursday	Visit Grandma	?
Friday	Go to the concert	?
Saturday	?	Clean the house
Sunday	?	Play basketball

Figure 10.5: Information gap diaries

Student A: 'What are you going to do on Wednesday?'

Student B: 'I'm going to swim in the river. What are you going to do on Monday?'

Student A: 'I'm going to play football. What are you going to do on Saturday?'

36. Ordering words to make a correct sentence

Materials: none.

Compose a very short sentence of only five or six words, for example, 'Shazia gave me a present'. Call out five or six students to go outside the classroom with you. Now tell these students that each of them is a word in this sentence. For example, one student is 'gave', one is 'Shazia', one is 'present', one is 'me' and one is 'a'. Now tell these students to stand in front of the class in an incorrect order. Each must say their own word clearly to the whole class. Now invite a student in the class to move one person so that the sentence is more correct. Other students continue moving one 'word' at a time until the word order of the sentence is correct.

Figure 10.6: Students doing a word-order activity

Now invite any student to think of their own word which can be added to the sentence and to come up to the front and join the sentence. The sentence must always remain correct. For example, 'Shazia gave me a BEAUTIFUL present'. Students can also discuss ideas together and come up in pairs or groups to add phrases to the sentence, for example, 'Shazia gave me a beautiful present FOR MY BIRTHDAY'. Try to encourage all the students to participate by suggesting parts of speech (for example, adverb: VERY beautiful present) or indicating where a word could be added. Each time the sentence expands, ask the students to repeat the whole sentence to check that it is correct.

This activity is suitable for all levels. At advanced levels, it is a useful way of showing how simple sentences can be expanded with more information by inserting relative clauses, or making the sentence compound or complex. For example, 'As it was my birthday yesterday, Shazia gave me a beautiful present which she had bought in the market where her uncle sold jewellery which his wife made'.

After this activity, students can form groups and think of the longest sentence they can and write it on a long strip of paper. Now cut the paper into pieces with individual words and mix them up. Groups exchange their pile with another group which has to put the words in the correct order.

10.4 PRACTISING FUNCTIONAL LANGUAGE

Practising new functional language can be done in just the same way as practising new grammatical structures and new vocabulary. Don't forget, however, that one function can be expressed in many ways. For example, the function of asking someone to do something is expressed differently depending upon the relationship of the two speakers or upon how difficult the task is (see Section 9 for the presentation of functional language).

1. Fancy seeing a film on Thursday? (informal)

2. Would you like to go to a film on Thursday? (neutral)

3. I was wondering if you'd like to go to a film on Thursday. (formal)

Controlled activities for practising functional language

37. *Inviting and refusing*

Materials: flash cards with pictures of people doing leisure activities.

In a large class, quickly draw these on the board or fix the flash cards to the board and point to these when you want students to respond.

Ask two students who speak English well to practise the drill with you.

Example:

Teacher:　(indicating a card showing people playing football): 'Would you like to play football tomorrow?'

Figure 10.7: Flash cards

Student A: (as teacher indicates a card showing a festival): 'No, I'd prefer to go to the festival.' (Speaking to Student B): 'Would you like to go to the festival tomorrow?'

Student B: (as teacher shows a card showing a TV): 'No, I'd prefer to watch television.'

Now all students practise this while you indicate the pictures or hold up different flash cards. Later, students repeat this in groups. Later still, they can personalize what they would like to do.

Less controlled and guided activities for practising functional language

38. Persuading and refusing

Materials: none.

Finding adjectives to describe a favourite object could be the warmer for this activity.

Present the language of persuasion and refusing through listening.

Students work in pairs. One student, A, of each pair thinks about the most precious object that he/she owns and describes it to his/her partner B. Now B asks to buy this object, using the language of persuasion. A has to refuse, using the language of refusing. Give students only about one minute to do this activity. Then check how many Bs managed to persuade As and how many As managed to refuse successfully.

Language of persuasion: 'Would you mind . . . ', 'Could you possibly . . . ', 'Why not . . . ?', 'Why don't you . . . ?', 'Wouldn't it be better to . . . ?'

Language of refusal: 'I'm sorry but . . . ', 'I can't because . . . ', 'I'd like to, but . . . ', .

Other topics:

▶ persuading someone to study something they don't like.
▶ persuading someone NOT to do something they want to do (for example, get married very young, buy something very expensive, resign from their job, leave school).

39. Requesting

Materials: a collection of objects from the classroom or interesting things you or your students have brought. The students must know the names of these things in English.

Place the objects where most students can see them. Ask one good student to come to the front of the class. Now ask for one of the items, for example, 'May I have the scarf?'. The student answers, 'Yes, of course,' and gives the item to you. Continue asking for items and accepting them. After a few times, change places with the student. Give the item to another student in the class and then practise, 'May I have the scarf?', and 'I'm sorry, I don't have it'. You can also ask for things that are not in the room, for example, 'May I have an elephant?' (laughter improves learning!).

40. Agreeing and disagreeing

Materials: small cards with a phrase written on them (see examples below).

In this activity, students discuss a topic or do a role play in small groups. There is one phrase on each card. Place cards face upwards so that all students in each group can read the phrases. Every time a student uses one of the phrases, she/he can take that card. You may need several cards with the same phrases.

Sample language:

Agreeing	**Disagreeing**
I quite agree.	I wouldn't say that.
I think you're right.	That's not how I see it.
That's a very good point.	I think you're wrong.
	I disagree.

Examples of topics for discussion or role play:

▶ Television is a bad influence on everyone.
▶ Poor people are happier than rich people.
▶ Everyone should be taught in English from the age of five.
▶ Women can never be equal to men in the business world.

41. Keeping going and interrupting

Materials: none.

Present the language of interrupting (see below). Students work in groups. One student chooses a topic and starts to talk about it. Other students in the group have to try to interrupt as often as possible. This could be a competitive activity, where students work in teams, trying to make as many interruptions as possible. Put a pile of stones in the middle of the group. Every time a student interrupts, he/she takes a stone.

Sample language:

Interrupting	**Returning to the topic**
Sorry, but . . .	Anyway, . . .
Excuse me for interrupting, but . . .	In any case, . . .
Could I ask something?	Where was I?
Can I ask a question?	To get back to what I was saying . . .

Examples of topics:

▶ Something frightening that happened to you recently.
▶ How you travel from your home to the nearest big city.
▶ A description of someone you really like and why (this could be a friend or someone famous, like an actor or a sportsperson).
▶ How to play a sport or game.

42. Tell me more

Materials: none.

The students work in pairs or small groups. One student begins to talk about a topic. The others have to listen and select something he/she says and ask for more information. The speaker gives this information and then once again someone can ask for more information. This is good practice in responding to unpredictable topics.

Example:

Student A: 'This weekend I went home to visit my cousins.'

Student B: 'Oh, where do your cousins live?'

Student A: 'They live in the country not far from here. They all work on their father's farm.'

Student C: 'That's interesting. What sort of farm is it?'

Student A: 'Well, they grow rice and they have two water buffaloes.'

and so on.

43. Conversation chains

Materials: the board.

On one side of the board, write a list of events which call for congratulations. Now discuss with the students the language you use to congratulate someone and how the conversation might proceed after that (a conversation chain). You can write this conversation chain on the board, for example:

Student A	**Student B**
Greet your friend ⟶	Greet your friend
Congratulate your friend ⟷	Respond. Give information
Express admiration ⟵	
Ask question ⟶	Respond
Confirm ⟵	Thank and say goodbye
Say goodbye ⟵	

Now let students practise congratulating each other about different events using some of the expressions you discussed.

Sample language:

Congratulating	**Responding**
'By the way, congratulations on . . .'	'Oh, thank you.'
'By the way, I hear you've . . .'	'Yes, I'm/we're delighted/so pleased.'
'That's wonderful.'	'Yes, at last.'
'You must be so pleased.'	'Yes, I am/we are.'
Follow-up questions	'Well, it'll make a big difference.'
'So, how are things going?'	

Possible topics for congratulations: passing an exam, obtaining a scholarship or a new job or a promotion, publishing a book, getting married, having a baby, buying a new house, going on a course, passing your driving test.

Other language for conversation chains: complimenting, starting a conversation with someone you don't know, asking for information on the telephone, arranging to meet someone, commiserating on a sad event.

44. Mixed functions

Materials: a game board and dice for each group, tokens (such as a small stone, seed or button) for each student, a task list.

If you don't have any dice, make a spinner by cutting out small six-sided shapes. Write the numbers 1 to 6 in the segments. Now place a match stick through the middle so that students can twirl the spinner (see Figure 10.8). The number showing when the card touches the table is the score for that student.

It is more economical to make empty game boards, which you can use to practise many different structures or functions. Write only numbers in each square. Or, you can draw the game board on the board and give each group one piece of paper and ask them to copy the game board onto it.

Make a task list for each group. You can write this on the board or on a poster where all students can see it. Or, you can ask each group to copy the task list to practise writing.

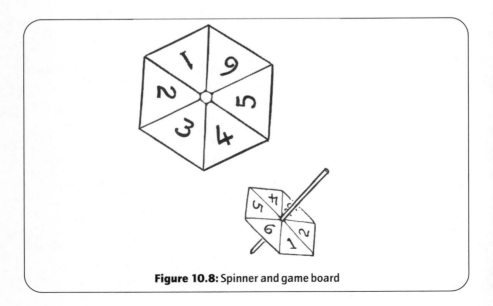

Figure 10.8: Spinner and game board

You can write the task list in the students' mother tongue as well as in English. Your tasks can focus on vocabulary, grammar or functional language, or on a mixture of all three, depending upon what you are practising.

To play the game, students work in groups of not more than six. Each student needs a small token, such as a stone, seed or button. They place these on square 1. Now the first student throws the dice or twirls the spinner, and moves his/her token forward the number of squares showing on the dice or spinner. For example, if his/her dice or spinner shows 3, he/she moves his/her token to land on square 3. He/she must now look up number 3 on the task list and follow the instructions.

Task list

Examples of tasks focusing on functional language:

1. Ask someone what their favourite food is and then agree or disagree with them.
2. Ask someone to lend you something.
3. Invite someone to go swimming with you.
4. Compliment someone on their clothes.

Examples of tasks focusing on vocabulary:

5. Name three red things.
6. Name three things beginning with B.
7. Name three items used in cooking.
8. Name three ways of walking.

Examples of tasks focusing on grammar:

9. What is the plural of box?
10. What is the simple past of the verbs 'to begin', 'to light', and 'to skip'?
11. Name the opposites of these: tall, heavy, long, dark.
12. Make this sentence active: 'I was taught cooking by my mother'.

45. Practising the correct level of formality

Materials: the board or flash cards.

Write several functional phrases which express one function on the board. For example: asking someone to do something.

▶ Could you . . . ?
▶ Would you mind . . . ?
▶ Could I ask you to . . . ?
▶ I wonder if you'd mind . . . ?
▶ Sorry to trouble you, but I wonder if you'd mind . . . ?

First, discuss with students which phrases are informal, neutral or formal. Now, write on the board or hold up flash cards saying, 'You and your brother' or 'You and your friend/boss/aunt/supervisor/teacher'. (You don't have to use flash cards, you can also call out the words yourself.) For each relationship, students have to choose an appropriate beginning to the sentence and finish the sentence using the appropriate level of formality (see pages 64–5 for phrases and ideas for other functions).

This activity can also be done in groups. One student reads a relationship from the board and another student gives the correct sentence. The rest of the group discusses whether the phrase is acceptable.

Variation 1: ask three students to come to the front of the class. Give each student a flash card with a character written on it. For example, one card says 'friend', another says 'teacher' and another says 'prime minister'. Now other students in the class have to ask one of the three characters to do something, using one of the functional phrases (the students must specify which character they are speaking to). Only the student whose character corresponds to the functional phrase must do the action. So, for example, a student can ask, 'Prime minister, could you help me?'. 'Could you' is an informal phrase which is not appropriate for speaking to the prime minister, so the student whose character is the prime minister does not move. Instead, the student whose character is 'friend' offers to help.

Variation 2: phrases asking someone to help or to do something become longer if the task is more demanding. For example: 'Could you post this letter for me?' (an easy task), or 'I'm sorry to trouble you, but I wonder if you'd mind driving my brother to hospital?' (a more demanding task). You can do similar activities to practise this aspect of the function of asking people to help.

Remember that functional language can also be practised by using substitution drills, questionnaires and information gap activities.

In this section, the sample activities illustrate many possibilities for practising new language.

Remember that you can:

▶ use activities to practise new grammar, vocabulary or functional language, or pronunciation;

▶ control activities quite strictly and place emphasis on accuracy, or you can only guide activities so that students have more choice in the language they use;

▶ change the level and topic of activities according to your students' needs and abilities;

▶ use different interaction patterns according to the number of students in your class;

▶ do choral drilling with the whole class or with only half of the class. You can drill around the classroom or choose students at random. Students can also practise in pairs and in groups of up to six;

▶ use different materials to cue or prompt the activities: the board, flash cards, small cards, the students themselves, students' own ideas and opinions, buttons, stones, objects in the classroom or objects brought in from outside.

Once students have had an opportunity to practise speaking during the Practice phase, they should be ready to concentrate on speaking fluently with little direction from the teacher. This is the Production phase of the lesson. During this phase, students focus on becoming more fluent. Your task is to prepare the students well during the Presentation and Practice phases and to set up interesting and motivating activities, followed by useful feedback and correction, for the Production phase.

In the next section, you will find ways which help you to do this.

11 / The Production Phase: Speaking Fluently

11.1 THE PRODUCTION PHASE OF A PPP LESSON ON SPEAKING

After the Practice phase, when students practise using language *accurately*, they have to practise using language as *fluently* as possible. This is the Production phase. The Production phase is the last stage of a PPP lesson. You can also focus a whole lesson upon using English fluently, in which case the whole lesson is like a Production phase. The Production phase can also be called the fluency phase or the free phase.

In the Production phase, language learners concentrate upon using recently learnt grammar, functional language and vocabulary with fluency when they speak. Fluency means speaking with ease and without thinking about possible errors. We all speak our first language fluently and we do not worry about mistakes, but concentrate on communicating what we want to say.

During fluency activities, the students concentrate on using all the English they know in order to communicate their message and to understand other speakers. They will make some mistakes, but now you do not correct them as you did earlier in the Practice phase. This gives your students a chance to experiment using the language they have learnt to communicate in a way that is similar to using English in real life.

In this section, we give many sample activities to help students become more fluent.

It is important that your students can practise speaking fluently in a supportive classroom. So first of all, let's look at three important areas to help you manage fluency activities in the Production phase:

► good preparation and support;
► students' interest in the topic;
► other people's attitudes to fluency activities.

Good preparation and support

During the Production phase, students will speak with little help from you, so the language they say and hear is more unpredictable. This is why they need good preparation and support before the Production phase to help them do this successfully.

For example, if students are asked to place ideas in a certain order (ranking activities) or to group ideas into categories (categorizing activities), they need to know the functional language of agreeing and disagreeing. The kinds of phrases they will need are:

► 'Yes, you're right.'
► 'I agree with the first part, but ...'
► 'I disagree because ...'.

They will also need appropriate vocabulary to talk about the topic. For example, if they are ranking their preferences of the jobs they would like to do when they leave school, they need to know the names of different professions.

To build your students' confidence, you can suggest that they can use their first language for a group discussion about the activity. Then, they can tell the class or other groups about their ideas in English. This is particularly helpful if they have to speak about complex ideas. They can gather their ideas easily and quickly in their first language, and then communicate them in English to the rest of the class.

Some students do not like taking part in fluency activities, so they are not able to join in a conversation easily. Other students may be reluctant to participate because they are afraid of making mistakes. These students can be encouraged to overcome their fears if you give lots of language preparation before the Production phase. Also, explain that making mistakes is part of the learning process. We all sometimes make small mistakes when we speak in our first language, but these small mistakes do not prevent other people from understanding us. So they should not worry about making some mistakes when they are speaking English to practise fluency.

Sometimes, students may have difficulty understanding what others are saying to them. Encourage students to look at the person who is speaking. You can also teach the functional language of clarification, so they can use English phrases to ask for clarification. For example:

► 'Can you say that again, please?'
► 'Sorry, I don't understand'.

To help your students to remember these useful phrases, ask them to write the phrases on a poster that everyone can see easily.

During the activities, walk quietly around the classroom, listening and watching. Encourage students to carry on speaking without worrying about their mistakes. When students ask you for help, try to guide them rather than correcting them or giving them the exact answer.

If you find several students make the same mistake or are having problems, make a note of these. Later in the lesson, you can write common mistakes on the board. Encourage the class to discuss them and try to elicit (see page 58) the correct answers. You can then ensure that everyone knows the correct answers.

Students work in pairs and groups for fluency activities, so it is important to make sure that all, or most, of the students are happy in their groups. You can do this by:

▶ changing the groupings regularly to provide variety for the students. This can help if students are unhappy within a particular group.

▶ placing quiet and confident students in separate groups. This gives the quiet and less confident speakers more opportunities to contribute. In mixed groups, make sure that groups support the less confident speakers.

▶ asking students to form their own groups (but this needs careful management to ensure that all students, including the quieter ones, can participate).

▶ giving each student in each group a role, for example, 'secretary' for less confident speakers, which gives them something to say. If you give noisy or confident speakers a role that involves writing, you can discourage them from dominating a group.

Students' interest in the topic

Try to choose topics that are relevant and appropriate to your learners' experience, for example, if they are very young, or they do not have access to television or to a computer, or they have not travelled far from their village.

Think about how you can personalize the information in your course book to make it relevant to your students' life experience. For example, if your course book mentions aeroplane flights and none of your students has been on an aeroplane, talk about bus or train travel instead. If the book mentions towns in England, replace these with cities in the students' own country.

Your students may be interested in learning about a particular topic so that they can talk about it during fluency activities. Ask other teachers about the topics in their subject syllabus and see if you could use them for fluency activities.

Other people's attitudes

In all the speaking activities which follow, we have suggested topics which are quite conventional. This is because most students will know about and feel happy to speak about everyday topics. But you do not have to follow our suggestions. You can think of your own topics. And one of the best ways to motivate students and encourage them to speak is to ask them which topics they want to speak about.

If your students have enough English, they may wish to speak about topics which could be seen as controversial. For example, students may want to speak about bullying, or adult learners may wish to discuss political or social topics which may be sensitive.

A controversial topic can be an excellent motivation for students to become really involved in a discussion and communicate fluently in English. However, some cultures do not always encourage individual opinions, or expect young people to disagree with their elders or to comment on community issues.

You will know what topics are acceptable in your community and you can play a role in ensuring that topics and discussions are acceptable. A practical way of doing this is to make groups single sex, close in age or from the same community.

But remember also that it is good experience for students to find out about speaking habits in other cultures, particularly if they may be going to study, work or visit English-speaking countries. You are the best person to decide which topics are appropriate for your class.

How to manage speaking activities

Here are some tips to help you manage and organize fluency speaking activities:

▶ Make sure that the students have practised the necessary grammar and vocabulary before they start the activity.
▶ Place students into pairs or groups quickly and without a fuss (see page 32).
▶ Explain the activity and write instructions on the board.
▶ Tell students how much time they have to do the activity.
▶ Demonstrate the activity with one pair or group in front of the whole class if necessary.

▶ Encourage another pair or one group to stand up in front of the class to demonstrate the activity.
▶ During the activity, monitor the work and quieten noisy students.
▶ Make sure all students participate for at least part of the lesson.
▶ Listen for mistakes and note them down, so you can correct them later. Do not correct errors during the activity.
▶ Help weaker students.
▶ Give a clear signal to end the activity.
▶ Give and/or ask for feedback on the activity.

We have grouped the sample activities for the Production phase into four categories:

▶ sharing information;
▶ solving problems;
▶ projects and presentations;
▶ role plays.

These categories help you work with different activity types, although some activities fall into more than one category. You can adapt most of these sample activities for different age groups and different language levels if you:

▶ adapt the topic to something that is suitable to the age and level of your students, from younger children to adult learners;
▶ give students more preparation before the activity;
▶ help students more during the activity;
▶ allow students different time limits to do the activity.

We suggest some variations (different ways of doing the activities or different topics) to show you how activities can be adapted. These are not the only possible variations, and we encourage you to find your own ways of adapting the activities.

We also mention specific resources which you need to prepare in advance. But don't worry, the preparations are easy and do not take much time.

We do not give any suggestions as to how long the activities will take, because this depends on you and your students. The way you manage the activity and how easy or interesting the students find it affects how long the activity takes. However, we think that you can fit each of these activities into the time that you have, and the timing of the different parts of your lesson can be flexible.

Many of the sample speaking activities below can be followed by a writing activity. Depending on the type of speaking activity, students could do one of these writing activities:

▶ a report on a group's findings or ideas;
▶ a letter to a newspaper;
▶ a class profile (or questionnaire);
▶ filling in some pages in a diary.

11.2 SHARING INFORMATION

The activities in this section give students a lot of practice with repeated questions which they can answer in any way they like.

Sharing in pairs

46. *Favourites*

Materials: none.

Students ask each other about their favourite food, favourite book, favourite film or favourite place to visit. The activity can be very free if you do not give the class any language or question types. However, if your students need more help, you can give them a conversation outline like this one:

Student A: 'What's your favourite book?'

Student B: '*Things Fall Apart.*'

Student A: 'Why do you like it?'

Student B: 'I like it because . . . '

Variation: sports and games.

Students ask each other:

Student A: 'Do you like (playing chess)?'

Student B: 'Yes I do.'/'No I don't.'

Student A: 'Why do you like (playing chess)?'

Student B: 'I like it because . . .'

Questionnaires (pairs or groups)

47. *Characteristics*

Materials: the board and students' notebooks.

Ask students to give you characteristics of people, for example, energetic, outgoing, shy, etc. Write their suggestions on the board, and then ask students to include these words in a short questionnaire. For example:

Student A: 'Are you (lazy)?'

Student B: 'Yes'/'Maybe'/'Sometimes'/'Don't know'/'No'.

Variation: habits.

Students ask each other questions such as:

▶   Do you get up early?
▶   Do you watch a lot of TV?

Regrouping (different groups)

48. The whole story

Materials: a text which has been divided up and written on small cards.

Divide the class into groups. Give each member of the group a card with part of a story so that between all the group members, they have the complete story. Each student in the group reads their part of the story and they speak about what they have read with each other. Then, take away the texts and ask students to retell their part of the story to their group.

If you have enough space in your classroom, you can then change the original groups into new groups. Make sure that each new group has one representative from each of the first groups. These are sometimes called 'jigsaw' groups. Each student tells the new group their part of the story, and together they sort out the order of the whole story.

For example, divide a story into six parts and then divide the students into six groups. Give all the students in one group a letter, A, B, C, D, E or F, etc, depending upon how many groups there are. So the first grouping is: AAAA, BBBB, CCCC, DDDD, EEEE, FFFF.

Then, after the discussion, ask students to make new groups, with one representative from each original group in each new group. So, the new grouping is: ABCDEF, ABCDEF, ABCDEF, ABCDEF.

Often, there is a different number of groups for the second grouping than for the first grouping. This example is for a class of 24 students. If, for example, you have 48 students continue to name them using the letters A2, B2, C2, D2, E2 and F2.

If you do not have space to move around, you can exchange the different group information in stages. Two students leave their own group and visit another group, where they retell their part of the story. When they have finished, two other group members visit other groups to pass on their part of the story. These 'messengers' take turns to visit other groups, until all groups have been visited.

49. General knowledge

Ask each student to research two or three general knowledge questions and answers. Make sure you check their information. Ask them to write each question and answer on one piece of paper, and then to write each of their questions only on a separate piece of paper.

Hand out the question papers between groups of three or four students, but make sure that you do not give them their own questions! The groups try to answer the questions they have. Then use the 'messenger' process (see above) to transfer the answers to all groups. This activity is more suitable for more advanced students.

11.3 SOLVING PROBLEMS

These activities give students a chance to practise language that they know, but they have to think about how to solve the situation they are given and what they will say.

Predicting

50. What happens next?

Materials: a text of a story, such as a newspaper report of a local incident. It should not be a well-known traditional story.

Read out the first part of the story, which introduces the beginning of the story and the characters. Ask the students to discuss the story and predict what happens next. The predictions can be acted out for other groups or for the class.

Variation: picture story.

Instead of reading a text, show a picture which tells part of a story. Ask the students to predict what happens next. The predictions can be acted out for other groups or for the class.

Modifying

51. Thinking differently

Materials: the board.

On the board, write a set of statements about family and community life which are acceptable in your culture, but which will generate some debate. For example:

▶ Children should always do what their parents tell them.
▶ Going to prison is good for all criminals.
▶ Lots of money makes people happy.

Students work in pairs or small groups and discuss these statements. Ask them to add or change words so that the statements reflect the beliefs of the whole group, for example,

▶ Children UNDER 12 YEARS OLD should USUALLY do what their parents tell them.

Variation: it's important to me (ranking activity).

Write on the board a list of values, such as: family, health, wealth, success. In pairs, students discuss and agree the order of importance of these topics in their life. Then, students work in groups of four and again discuss the importance of the values. They have to agree an order of importance. Finally, if there is time and space, students work in groups of eight and come to a final agreement on the order of importance. A representative from each group can report back to the rest of the class on the group decision.

Ordering

52. Making connections

Materials: a picture story.

Find a picture story without words, or use a picture story in a comic magazine where you can cover the words. Alternatively find some pictures or advertisements from a magazine which show people, places and various objects.

Ask the students to work in pairs or small groups to talk about the pictures and to make a story by placing the pictures in a logical order. A representative from each pair or group can then tell their story to the whole class or to another pair or group. Remember that students may think of different but logical orderings of the pictures.

53. Describe and draw

Materials: students' workbooks.

Draw a picture (but keep it hidden from the students) that includes features such as a hill, a river, trees, flowers, clouds, houses, people and animals.

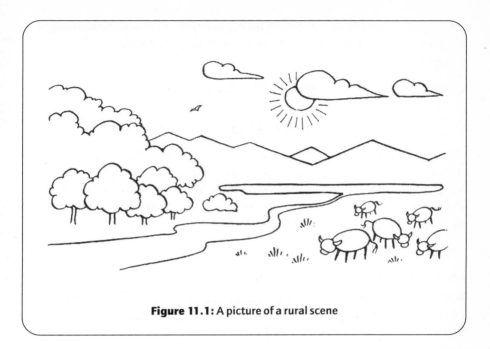

Figure 11.1: A picture of a rural scene

Describe this picture, step-by-step, using language such as:

► There are two . . .
► There is a . . . near the . . .
► In front of the . . . , there is a . . .

Ask the class to draw the picture as you describe it. Do not forget to pause often to give students time to draw. Then ask them to compare the pictures they have drawn.

Next, in pairs or small groups, one student draws a different picture, for example, a room, a house, a street scene, a scene in the garden or in the forest. In a similar way, they describe their picture, allowing time for the other students to draw. Afterwards they compare their interpretations. Students in pairs or groups can take turns to draw a picture and describe it.

Selecting

54. Holiday choice

Materials: the board.

Ask students to think of several local places they would like to visit for a day trip or for a weekend visit. Write these destinations on the board. Students first decide individually which is their favourite holiday destination. Then, in pairs, they discuss why they selected their place to visit.

Variation: imaginary destinations.

Students repeat the activity, this time with imaginary holiday destinations.

11.4 PROJECTS AND PRESENTATIONS

Projects and presentations sound as if they are difficult and long, and require a lot of research. However, they don't have to be. You can ask students to do a small project or short presentation within one lesson using the ideas below. The speaking activities can be done from a small to a large scale, lasting from one lesson to one term.

55. My favourite animal

Materials: poster-sized sheets of paper.

Most students have a favourite animal, either a pet, a farm animal or an animal that they have seen in the countryside, in a book, in a film or in a zoo.

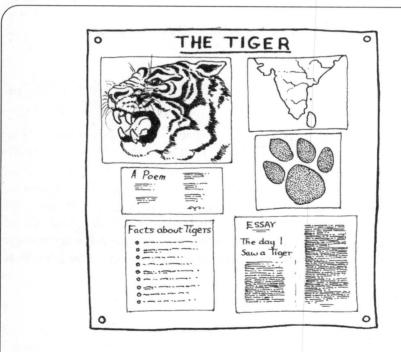

Figure 11.2: A poster of a presentation on tigers

Ask students to find or draw pictures of their favourite animal, together with some facts or opinions in written or graph form. You may need to show students different ways to present all this information. They could include drawings, photographs, maps, diagrams, poems and stories.

The final results can be displayed in the classroom, a school corridor or a meeting room. Your students then stand next to their animal projects and give a short talk (three to four minutes) about their favourite animal, or they answer questions from other students. This presentation can be given to other students in their class, or to other students in the school.

You can adapt the topic to suit the age and level of your learners. So, for example, older students can talk about their favourite sportspeople, and adult learners can talk about their favourite place to study or shop.

If some of your students are particularly nervous about standing up and speaking, they can present to a small group of class members.

Variation: my village/town/city.

This variation can be done in small groups, with each person concentrating on a different aspect of the village/town/city. The group needs to co-operate in planning and preparing the project or presentation.

56. A class trip

Materials: poster-sized sheets of paper.

Students work in small groups to discuss and plan a day trip for their class. They need to think about:

► how they will reach the destination;
► transport costs;
► possible entry fees;
► what students will do there;
► what students will report on when they return to class.

To make the project realistic, each group could present their ideas to the class. Then students can vote for their favourite trip, and that trip could be organized, if this is possible.

Variation: an English club.

Students plan an English club, discussing when and where it meets, and what activities they could use to improve their English, without a teacher.

57. *The park*

Materials: poster-sized sheets of paper, or a sand box and found items.

In this project, students discuss and plan their ideal park. They can plan the park using a drawing or by making a simple three-dimensional model using a cardboard box and some earth, or by using an area of earth outside the school.

You can either designate a specific area in your local community for an ideal park, or you can just give the students the size of a piece of land on which they can plan their park.

In groups of four to six, students have to decide first what facilities their ideal park will have. Then they have to plan which facilities go where and why. They need to think about access and safety, and an interesting and workable layout. Next, students make a drawing or a model of their ideas, which can be displayed in the classroom or in a school corridor or meeting room. Each group stands in front of their work and they either give a three to four minute talk about their design, or they answer questions about their design.

Variation: an ideal school/home/sports ground/garden.

This project can be done in the same way using different things to design.

58. *Public speaking*

Materials (optional): a box of objects from around the school or brought in by students.

Students take turns to stand up and present ideas on a topic of their choice. They need to prepare their talks. They can make notes and refer to them while they speak, but they should not read the presentation word for word.

The first time you do this activity, the talks can be only one to two minutes long, and as your students' confidence improves, the talks can last longer, up to five minutes. Other students then ask the speaker questions after their presentation.

You can have a box of objects which you or the students have brought in. Then, if a student cannot think of their own topic, they can take an object from the box and speak about that. They could talk about how it works, what it is used for or simply tell a story about what it reminds them of.

Variation: talking about themselves.

Students who are particularly nervous of standing up and speaking can speak to a small group of class members. They could speak about things they know about to help give them confidence, such as music, a sport they are good at or they like or local customs or crafts.

59. Discussion

Materials: none.

Students sit and face each other in groups of three to six, and discuss a topic (you can suggest it, or the students can choose their own). Students have to communicate their own ideas, opinions or stories. More advanced and older students can discuss more complex topics such as the role of women in society, or the role of multinational companies and global trade in development.

Students can also use this activity to practise functional language, such as interrupting or asking for clarification. However, a short time limit encourages students to speak with more focus.

Younger students may benefit from giving and listening to feedback from other groups. If students know that they will have to report on what they speak about, it can focus their discussion.

60. Book review

Materials: none.

When all the class has read a particular book, a discussion can be based on functional language such as giving opinions and agreeing and disagreeing with other people's opinions.

Variation: the class can discuss a film or play they have all seen.

11.5 ROLE PLAYS

In role plays, students act the part of a character in a particular situation. Give students cards which describe the situation and their character. Alternatively, students can create their own characters and choose the situation for a role play.

61. Four chairs

Materials: four chairs, stools or boxes to sit on.

Place four chairs at the front of the classroom. Ask students to suggest different arrangements of the four chairs to make different situations, for example:

▶ a car driver and three passengers (the car runs out of petrol and they have to decide what to do);

▶ four old schoolmates meet on a bus (they have not met for a long time);

▶ four strangers waiting for a job interview (they try to impress each other with their suitability for the job);

▶ a family in a restaurant (they argue over what is the best thing to eat);

▶ four friends meet after going to the cinema (they say whether they liked the film or not and why).

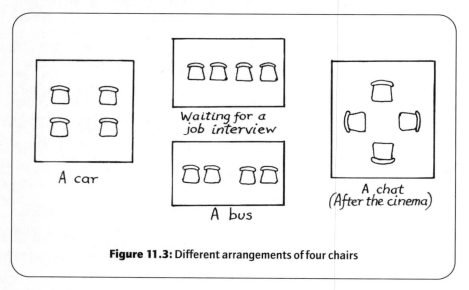

Figure 11.3: Different arrangements of four chairs

Variation: acting to the class.

Groups of four students plan and rehearse a dramatic scene for one of the above situations. Then some or all the groups sit on the chairs and present their drama to the class.

62. The interview

Materials: none.

In pairs, students act out a job interview, with one student (student A) asking questions about the other's (student B's) qualifications, experience and interest in the job, and student B answering. They can then change roles.

Variation: a famous person.

In pairs, one student acts the part of a famous person. The other student asks the famous person all the questions they have always wanted to ask. They can then change roles.

63. Factories and farmers

Materials: two posters.

Put up two posters on opposite sides of the classroom. One poster describes the situation and opinions of factory owners and the other poster describes the situation and opinions of farmers.

Factory owner: You own many successful factories and you want to build another factory near your village. You will employ many people in your new factory and you cannot understand why so many villagers are opposed to your plan.

Farmer: You do not want the new factory near your village. There will be a lot of noise and the river will be polluted, which will be bad for your crops and cattle.

Students work in pairs, one is a factory owner and the other is a farmer. They read the appropriate poster. They use the information and opinions to try to persuade the other to accept their point of view.

64. Reporter

Materials: newspapers.

Find, or ask students to find, suitable stories on TV, the radio, or in local newspapers. The story can be in English or in a local language but your students will speak about it in English. The stories could be about:

▶ disputes between people or organizations;
▶ an accident;
▶ different proposed plans for a new building.

The students work in pairs: one student acts as a newspaper reporter who interviews the other student about what happened. For example:

▶ when did it happen?
▶ who was there?
▶ where did it happen?
▶ how did it happen?

Variation: action scene.

Students act out these stories. They work in small groups and practise their stories before demonstrating them to another group in the class. Each group can do the same story or have a different story.

These sample activities show how your students can learn to communicate using all the English they know. With less guidance from you in this Production phase, they can become more fluent English speakers.

12 / Using a Text as a Basis for Speaking Activities

In this section, we show how you can use texts, including those in your course book, as a basis for speaking activities. You will see how these speaking activities will help your students understand and memorize the main points of a text, as well as helping them to expand their vocabulary and understand related grammar.

12.1 USING DIFFERENT TEXTS FOR SPEAKING ACTIVITIES

Many teachers and students have to use set course books. The lessons or units often start with a long text, which may not be very motivating or interesting for students. This text may be followed by comprehension questions and grammar exercises. Students are required to know this text well and to be able to complete the written exercises on it. So at first glance, the course book does not seem to be suitable for speaking activities.

We suggest sample speaking activities which you can use alongside or instead of the exercises in your course book. The speaking activities in this section will help students to memorize the main points of the text and to gain a good understanding of new vocabulary and grammar. Students will interact with the content of the text and discuss and appreciate the language. At the same time, they will have lots of speaking practice.

Why use a text?

A text is a very useful basis for a language lesson. It can provide a context for the lesson as well as language input.

However, in some learning situations, students focus only on translating and on memorizing the content and language in order to answer very specific questions in their examinations. This can be a useful exercise but it does not help students to speak English fluently.

In this section, we will show that a text is an excellent basis for a lesson or lessons using all four language skills: reading, writing, speaking and listening. The speaking activities show how you can use a text to improve reading, listening and speaking skills.

Types of texts

There are many types of text. Narrative texts with factual information are the easiest to use for speaking activities. We give some sample activities using narrative and factual texts. In addition, we also include sample speaking activities using dialogues and poetry. Some of the activities can be used for more than one type of text.

Even if your students have to work on set texts, it is always a good idea to collect other texts. Everything you read, in and out of the classroom, is a potential text. If you can, cut it out or copy it and store it carefully. It is helpful to categorize texts under headings like subject matter, level or suitability for certain activities.

Short stories or incidents from a newspaper can provide useful human-interest stories. You can translate these into English yourself if necessary. Maybe there are texts in other course books which you can use. Look out for recent texts on topics you have to study, as they may be more up to date than your course book. You can then compare these texts with the texts in your course book, for facts, style or language differences.

A text collection may be useful to other teachers in your school or in nearby schools too, so you could ask them to help you produce a collection of texts which you can all use.

12.2 GETTING THE TEXT ONTO THE BOARD

For some activities, you may need to write a text on the board so that students can copy it. Here is a way of doing this which gives students the chance to practise listening, speaking and writing instead of simply copying the text.

Read the first part of the text or the first key sentences to the class. Students listen, without taking notes. Now ask some questions about the text. The answers to these questions will help to reconstruct the text. Now write this first part of the text on the board, sentence by sentence. In this way, students only copy one or two sentences before they listen to the next part of the text and then answer the next set of questions. Continue this activity until the students have copied the whole text.

12.3 SAMPLE ACTIVITIES FOR A SPEAKING LESSON USING A NARRATIVE TEXT

Here is an example of a lesson focusing mainly on speaking which includes a range of activities based around a narrative text. It shows how you can use a text as the basis for a lesson which combines a flexible PPP framework with all four language skills, but with the emphasis upon speaking.

Some of the activities have a strong emphasis on the *language* used in the text. Others are based upon the *content*. Most of the time, you will not use all these activities to study one text, but we want to show you that one text can be the basis for many activities.

Sample text

Student's thirteen-day ordeal

Edouard Dubois is an eighteen-year-old chemistry student. Last year, he was riding his bike along the motorway when the wheel struck a boulder. He was thrown over the safety barrier and tumbled 30 feet into the ravine which ran beside the road. His left leg was broken and his right ankle badly twisted and he was unconscious for several minutes.

This motorway ran through a busy suburb of the city and was jammed with traffic most of the day. When he came to, Edouard realized that his cries for help would never be heard above the roar of the traffic, so he decided to crawl along the bed of the ravine, dragging his wounded leg behind him.

Luckily, Edouard had always had a passion for the outdoors and his knowledge of berries and leaves helped him to survive. He managed to collect some sips of water from the stream which meandered along the bottom of the ravine in order to quench his thirst. 'It was the sound of the birds which kept me going,' Edouard said when his ordeal was over.

Thirteen days after the accident, a M. Gilbert, whose house over-looked the ravine, was working in his garden when a figure appeared crying 'Help me! Help me!' His clothes were torn and bedraggled and his hair was unkempt. 'I thought he was a criminal,' said M. Gilbert. 'He staggered towards the hose and shoved it down his throat. My wife made some sandwiches, which he devoured in seconds, while I rang for an ambulance.'

Edouard's father is a well-known lawyer. He and his wife had given up hope of seeing their son alive again. 'He never stays out late,' they said, 'so, of course, when he wasn't home by the small hours, we reported him missing to the police. We were watching television when the hospital rang to say he was alive. You can imagine how overjoyed we were. We certainly underestimated his will to survive.'

(Anonymous)

Warmers

65. Word collecting

Do a word collection (see page 47). Ask some groups to find words for vegetation (bush, trees, grass, etc.) and other groups to write down as many words as possible for geographical features (hills, mountains, cliffs, ravine, river, stream, etc.).

66. Prediction

Write the title of the text on the board. First, students discuss in pairs or groups what they think the text is about. Then there can be a general class discussion.

Presentation phase

67. Pre-teaching essential vocabulary

This is quite an advanced text. Pre-teach between six and eight words which your students may not know (see page 60). Words which may be unfamiliar in this text are: boulder, ravine, tumble, jammed, berries, meander, bedraggled and unkempt.

Skills work: checking understanding

68. Listening or reading

Read the first paragraph of the story to the students. Or, if all the students have a copy of the text, ask them to read the first paragraph and then to look up. This way, you know when they are ready to listen to your checking questions.

69. 'Yes/No' questions

Test the students' understanding by asking 'yes/no' questions like those below. Students may only answer 'yes' or 'no'. Use some of the new vocabulary. For example:

▶ Was Edouard a mathematics student?
▶ Was he driving a car?
▶ Was he thrown over the safety barrier?
▶ Did he tumble 50 feet into a river?

70. *Open questions*

Now ask some open questions, where students must use the information and some of the language of the text in their answers. Here are some examples of open questions:

▶ Tell me about Edouard.
▶ What happened to his bike?
▶ What was he thrown over?
▶ How far did he tumble?

Practice phase: language work

71. *Grammatical analysis*

This text has many situations when the unreal conditional could be used, for example:

▶ If the wheel hadn't struck a boulder, Edouard would not have tumbled over the safety barrier.

Write this conditional sentence on the board and check that the students understand how the sentence is formed. Then erase the second half of the sentence after the comma. Ask the students to look through the story and to write a similar half sentence. They then exchange these half sentences with the person sitting next to them, who has to complete the sentence. The pairs can discuss whether each sentence is correct and some examples can be read out to the whole class.

These discussion activities can be done in pairs or groups. All the pairs or groups can do all the activities, or certain groups can work on different tasks at the same time.

72. *Grammar*

In pairs or groups, students discuss and then underline all grammar structures which show a past continuous used together with a past simple. (*Example:* He was riding [past continuous] . . . when his bike struck [past simple] a boulder.)

73. *Grammar*

Working in pairs or groups, students have to discuss and then underline the grammar structure of verb + preposition and phrasal verbs. (Example: He was thrown over . . . [verb + preposition]. When he came to [phrasal verb] . . .)

74. *Vocabulary*

Pairs or groups discuss and make a note of all words in the text which describe how Edouard moves (for example: riding, crawl, staggered).

75. *Vocabulary*

Pairs or groups have to find all the words which have the prefixes 'over' or 'under' (for example: overlooked, underestimated). Ask students to think of other expressions which use these prefixes.

76. *Vocabulary*

Pairs or groups have to find all words which express emotions. They can also include words which describe how the main character felt, even if they are not in the text.

Now let students report what they have found to the rest of the class and discuss the language in these activities.

Less controlled practice

77. *Retelling the story*

Draw the following flow chart (Figure 12.1) on the board and, with your students, fill in the boxes with appropriate verbs to recall the story from Edouard's point of view. When this is complete, do a similar chart with your students to tell M. Gilbert's story and then that of Edouard's mother and father.

These flow charts do not need to be absolutely accurate as long as the story is correct and the language used in the text is recycled correctly.

Production phase

78. *Fluency – role play*

Model a role play in which you play the part of a reporter and several good students take the parts of Edouard, M. Gilbert and his wife and Edouard's parents. When you have modelled this well, the rest of the class can do the role play in groups of six.

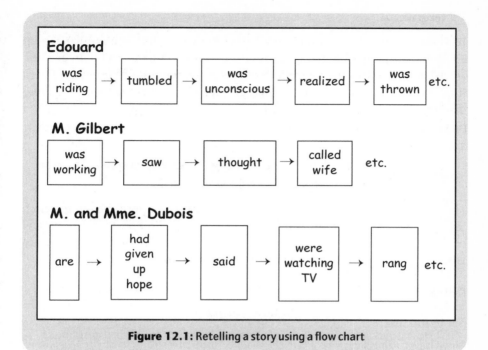

Figure 12.1: Retelling a story using a flow chart

79. *Production – writing*

If another activity is needed, students can write an article for the local newspaper or can pretend they are one of the characters and can write a letter describing the incident to a friend.

Other activities that can be used with narrative texts

80. *Personalization*

Choose a topic for a story that could have happened to one of your students, for example, a journey or a special day. Give students some time to prepare a short talk and ask them to tell the class or their group about their experience. If you do enough preliminary work, as in the sample lesson above, students should have enough vocabulary and structures to do this activity.

81. *Interviews*

If the text has one particularly interesting character, let the students prepare questions to interview that person. You can take the part of that person. Alternatively, let half the students write questions and half study the text well (and even expand on the information in the text) so that students can role play the interview in pairs.

82. *Ordering*

If you can copy the text several times (enough copies for each group), cut up each copy into separate paragraphs or sections and mix them up. In groups, students take one section each and read it out to the rest of the group. Then, they must decide the order of the paragraphs. This is very useful for studying discourse (how a text is put together to make a coherent story), which can be the basis of a classroom discussion.

12.4 SAMPLE ACTIVITIES FOR A SPEAKING LESSON USING A FACTUAL TEXT

Here is an example of a lesson focusing entirely upon speaking which includes a range of activities around a factual text. This text is quite typical of those found in many traditional English language course books. Again, you will not use all these activities to study the text.

Sample text

School subjects

The subjects in our school timetable were English Language, English Literature, Scripture, History, Geography, Arithmetic, Algebra, Geometry, Hygiene and Physiology, Physical Training, Drawing, Sewing and Singing.

In Arithmetic, we worked seemingly endless problems on stocks and shares, wallpapering a room and filling a bath-tub with hot and cold water. ('A bath can be filled by a cold water tap in ten minutes and by a hot water tap in 15 minutes. How long does it take to fill the bath if both taps are turned on?')

It was a very good mental exercise and much of what I studied I found extremely interesting, but how odd it all seems today to realize that much of what we were taught had little relevance to our daily life or experience. Local people hardly bought any stocks and shares as they do today and we poor kids really hadn't the foggiest idea of what stocks and shares really were. We had also never seen wallpaper. And we had no long baths but took our baths local-style, standing up and sloshing water from an earthenware jar over ourselves with a dipper.

In English lessons, we read all about snow and robin red-breasts. And in Hygiene, we had to write in an examination how a water cistern worked when most of us had never seen one.

During Physical Training periods, we were taught the English Maypole Dance and English folk dances like 'Pop Goes the Weasel', 'Epping Forest', 'Newcastle' and 'Merry, Merry Milkmaids'. We performed the Maypole Dance once as an exhibition on Sports Day and anyone who has done it knows what a tricky business it is to get all the ribbons plaited correctly. One mistake and the dancers could be disgraced for ever.

Sewing classes were our favourite periods as we could sit in groups and talk a lot. We did samples of chain stitch, satin stitch, feather stitch, herring-bone stitch, button-hole stitch, etc., embroidery on table runners, cross-stitch woollen purses – but not a single garment did we sew which would have been more practical and useful. Once a year, an English lady would come to inspect our needlework and woe betide the girls whose work was not presentable, for it was not displayed and they were banished to the toilets for the duration of the examiner's visit.

(Excerpt from '*Rainbow Round My Shoulder*' by Ruth Ho, in *Understand and Communicate*, G.L. Ngoh)

Figure 12.2: We worked on maths problems on stocks and shares, wallpapering a room and filling a bath tub with hot and cold water

Warmers

83. Word search

Make a word-search poster using the words of the subjects the writer studied at school (see page 52). In teams or pairs, the students must try to find the words.

84. Word collecting

Students work in groups to think of as many names of school subjects as they can. The group with the longest list wins.

85. Prediction

Ask the students to cover the text and to look only at the picture (Figure 12.2). They have to try to guess why the schoolgirls are puzzled by these topics.

86. Personalization

Ask students to work individually to write down the subjects they study. They must then rank them in the order of which they find most interesting or enjoyable. They can compare their list with their partner, explaining why they like particular subjects more than others.

Presentation phase

87. Pre-teach essential vocabulary

See page 60.

88. Reading for sense and discussion

Ask the students to read the whole text silently. Give them a time limit, so that they do not look up all the words they do not know. Ask them to close their books. In groups, ask them to list some of the difficulties the girls in the story had.

If the text is difficult for them, or if you only have one copy of the text, do this as a paragraph-by-paragraph reading or listening activity, with questions as in Activity 86 above. See also page 108 for tips on how to get a text on the board.

89. Language work

Students work in pairs and have to underline adverbs in the text, for example: seemingly, very, how, extremely, really, etc. This can form the basis for a discussion on adverbs which modify adjectives and those which modify verbs.

Practice phase: language work

90. Functional language: preparation for role play

Discuss with students the language they need to express opinions and how to agree and disagree in preparation for Activity 91.

Production phase

91. Production – role play

Ask students to work in groups to role play a meeting of school governors who have to decide which subjects will be studied. Tell them they must justify their choices and prepare to present them to the rest of the class. After each group has presented their choices, there can be a general class discussion to decide which subjects should be adopted.

92. Fluency – formal debate

Organize a formal debate or an in-class speaking competition on the subject of whether education today prepares students for real life.

93. Finding a title

This text has a hidden message about the relevance of education to students' real lives. Ask the students what they think the hidden message is. Ask them to choose a title that best describes the underlying intention of this piece of writing.

12.5 SAMPLE ACTIVITIES FOR A SPEAKING LESSON USING A DIALOGUE

Dialogues are samples of texts for speaking. Many courses require students to learn them from memory. This is useful if students understand what they are saying and if attention is paid to pronunciation. Here are some sample speaking activities for dialogues.

Sample dialogue

The star of the school

Yuri: 'Hi, Alexei, you look very smart. Where are you going?'

Alexei: 'Oh, these are the new team colours: green and yellow. I'm going to a team practice. Next Saturday, we are playing school No. 3. We'll have to work really hard. They're the best team in the district.'

Yuri:	'You are lucky. I'd love to play football for the school. But however hard I try, I never get picked for the team.'
Alexei:	'Perhaps I do more exercise than you. You need to be very fit to get selected.'
Yuri:	'The trouble is, my parents always want me to study, so I don't have much time left.'
Alexei:	'Well, you're much more clever than I am. There's no-one better than you at maths.'
Yuri:	'Who cares if you're good at maths? The people in the football team are always the most popular people.'
Alexei:	'Stop worrying. If you get to university, you'll be the star of the school!'
Yuri:	'And if you play in the World Cup, you'll be the richest person in town!'

Warmers

94. Prediction

Before the students see the text, write the title of the dialogue (or make one up yourself) on the board and let the students discuss the following points in pairs or groups:

▶ Who do you think takes part in this dialogue?
▶ Where do you think they are?
▶ What topics do you think they will talk about?
▶ Have you ever had a conversation with friends about this topic?

95. Discussion of controversial issues on the topic of the dialogue

Before letting the students read the title or the text of the dialogue, write three or four sentences on the board which will provoke discussion about the topic. For example:

▶ Study is more important than sport.
▶ Only people who are good at sport should have to do it at school.
▶ Competition is a bad thing and creates bad feelings.
▶ Everyone has some kind of talent which we should recognize.

Now students can discuss the topic in pairs or groups. Younger or weaker students can do this in their first language, but more advanced students can use English.

Presentation phase

96. Language work

Vocabulary: write six or eight synonyms (or antonyms) for some of the words in the dialogue on the board in a random order. In pairs or groups, students discuss these and match them to words in the dialogue.

Grammar: in pairs, students underline specific grammatical features within the dialogues, for example, comparatives. These can then form the basis for explanation or revision.

Example:

► 'The best team in the district.'
► 'Perhaps I do more exercise than you.'
► 'There's no-one better than you at maths.'
► 'The people in the football team are always the most popular people.'

97. Learning the dialogue

Some dialogues need to be shortened if the students have to learn them word for word. Write the dialogue on a poster and help students learn it by using the technique of disappearing dialogue (see page 76).

If students do not have to learn the dialogue word for word but have to know the content well, let them practise the conversation in pairs or groups, after they have done some language work. They can improvise by using whatever language they can to express the ideas in the dialogue. Pairs or groups then perform the dialogue to other groups or to the class.

Production phase

98. Discussion and role play

After studying the dialogue, encourage students to talk about the characters. They can start by finding adjectives to describe each character. Now, encourage students to envisage another scene in which these characters take part (maybe a situation after the events in the dialogue). Each group should plan and practise their own alternative dialogue and act it out to other groups or to the whole class. They can write and learn it, or more advanced students can improvise.

12.6 SAMPLE SPEAKING ACTIVITIES FOR POEMS

Most poetry work focuses upon the content of the poem, rather than upon new grammar or language. The discussions about content and meaning can be in the students' first language, and more advanced students can use English.

Many of the activities for texts above also can be used to encourage students to speak about poems, for example, predicting the content from the title or a picture, or discussing controversial statements on the topic of the poem. You can also use the disappearing dialogue technique (see page 76) if students have to learn the poem from memory. For longer narrative poems, you can use some of the activities suggested for a narrative text.

In addition to the activities in previous sections, the following activities bring variety to the lesson and help students gain a fuller understanding of the text.

Poem A is best used with lower level students or with younger learners.

Poem A: 'Mothering a Mouse'

Once upon a happy day
A dew-eyed mouse found her way
Into Zoe's home.

Zoe with embracing care
lifted mousy from her snare
and popped her in a box.

Central to the scientist's gaze
mousy made a tiny maze –
a cosy place to snooze.

Each day, she surfaced for a preen
her silken fur was made to gleam,
and her smooth tail too.

Zoe watched and wrote the story
of this creature's living glory
in an article.

Then she released mouse far away.
In the wild, she is to stray
where freedom reigns.

(Dee Uprichard, 1992)

99. Gap fill

Write Poem A on a poster or handout, leaving out several key words, for example: 'way', 'care', 'maze', 'snooze', 'gleam', 'tail', 'story' and 'away'. In pairs, students try to guess what the missing words might be. They can then discuss their predictions. If they are wrong, talk about why the poet chose these particular words.

If missing words are too difficult for your students, write the correct words on the board in random order and let the students discuss with their partners or groups where these words should go.

100. Speaking about the content of the poem

Talk to the students about Zoe, for example,

► Is she the poet? If not, who is she?
► Why did Zoe save the mouse?
► How do we know that she likes the mouse?
► Why did she let it go?

Now ask students to think of animals (domestic or wild) that come into their houses, like frogs, geckos, spiders, dogs, cats, lizards, etc. Each student chooses an animal and talks about what they do when these animals come into their house. Do they want to keep the animal? How would they look after it? Are they afraid of the animal? Would they release it?

101. Language work

Ask students to underline words or phrases that describe the mouse. Then they have to think of adjectives to describe the animal they have chosen to talk about. They should do this in pairs or groups and help each other.

More advanced students often find it interesting to compare two poems. Here are two more poems about animals and some suggestions of how students can study these through speaking activities. You can also choose your own two poems. After you have done this activity, more advanced students can write their own poems on a selected topic and you can use this as the basis for similar activities.

Poem B: 'Sunset'

warm scent
lingers
to mark his passage
through

leaves and flowers
breathing
perfume
as under
the surveillance of
furtive eyes
he
buries
his mane
of fire
in the darkness
of his paws
and
with
bloodshot eyes
stalks
into the grass

birds
twitter
with anxiety
as the predator

comes
to take
his place
for the night.

Poem C: 'Snake'

The slithering coil contorts
Quickly from shade to shade
Sliding moistly on shining scales.

The black wire tongue darting
From the arrogant head, with tiny eyes,
Stings through the lush, hot grass

And the birds rise in shrieking chaos,
As the urgent spectre, in its shroud
Of fear and dark beauty, disappears.

Under an arching braid of twisting roots
Into the hollow of its secret home
Cool in the soft dampness of the earth.

(From 'Shade in Passing', by G.F. Riaz, 1991).

102. Brief comparison of the two poems

Write some questions on the board or on a poster which promote a comparison of the two poems. Students discuss these questions in pairs or groups.

Sample questions:

► Which animals are the poems about? Why did you guess this?
► What do the two poems have in common?
► What are the main differences?

103. Language work and discussion

These activities are done in pairs. Either let pairs of students work on both poems or half the class can work on Poem B in pairs and the other half on Poem C. Then regroup so that new pairs can exchange their responses to their individual poems. Then have a discussion of both poems as a class.

Working in pairs:

► Find and underline the words which describe the physical appearance of the animals.
► Write down the words which show how the animals move. Why do you think the poets chose these words?
► How do the birds react to the animals?
► You know about one animal's resting place. What do you think the other is like?
► Which poem describes the animal better? Why do you think this?

104. Personal response to the poems: writing and class discussion

Write the following on the board:

► I like poem B/C because . . .
► I don't like poem B/C because . . .
► Write anything you want to (one or two sentences) about one or both of these poems.

Working in pairs, students complete the sentences individually and then discuss their responses with their partners. Write some responses on the board and use these as the basis for a class discussion of the poems.

In a small class or in groups, students could write their responses to the suggestions above on a small piece of paper which is folded and placed in a bowl in the middle of the class or group. These are then unfolded one by one, read and discussed by the class or group.

13 / Pronunciation

In this section, we look at ways to improve your students' pronunciation of English to help other speakers of English understand them better. We describe a variety of short activities which practise pronunciation and which you can easily fit into any lesson.

13.1 WHAT IS PRONUNCIATION?

A speaker's pronunciation needs to be good enough to communicate the message so that it is understood by other speakers of English.

There are many acceptable varieties of English. The sounds you and your students recognize and speak is the variety of English which is spoken in your country or region.

It does not matter if your students speak Nigerian English or Bangladeshi English or any of the many other varieties of English spoken around the world. What *is* important is mutual intelligibility: can other speakers of English understand your students' English, and can your students understand the English they hear?

Some language learners think they have to sound like a native speaker of a particular variety of English, but this is not necessary. The most important thing is that your students understand people speaking English, and that they can be understood by other speakers of your local variety of English. If your students need to talk with speakers of English in another part of the world, they need to be prepared that the English may sound slightly different.

Sounds of English

Spoken standard English has 44 sounds, but there are only 26 letters in the alphabet for written English. This can make pronouncing some English words a bit difficult, because the sounds and the spelling do not always match.

However, effective English pronunciation is not only about making correct individual sounds. Language learners also need to know:

▶ the sounds of spoken English;
▶ which parts of a word are more heavily stressed, that is, spoken louder and longer;
▶ which part or parts of a sentence can be more heavily stressed;
▶ how to link the sounds together in a sentence;
▶ basic intonation, that is, up and down sound patterns;
▶ what it means to change the intonation in a sentence.

Language learners need practice in all these areas to improve their English pronunciation.

Recognition before practice

Repeating new sounds in a new language can be a challenge for language learners. It is particularly difficult for speakers of a language that does not have the same sounds as English. So to help your students become better speakers of English, you need to give your students the opportunity to listen and recognize what they have heard before they try to repeat it.

If your students have difficulties in saying certain sounds in English, you can help them to recognize these sounds more easily if you:

▶ say the new word clearly on its own several times;
▶ say the new word in a sentence several times, while indicating with your hand in the air when you say the new word;
▶ explain how to produce the sound in your students' first or main language and what to do with the tongue and teeth. You can demonstrate this if you use the curve of your hand to represent the roof of your mouth, and keep the other hand flat like your tongue. You could also make a simple drawing of the mouth on the board;
▶ contrast the new sound with a known sound, and help students to hear the difference by saying these two sounds alternately.

The needs of young learners and adult beginners

Teaching pronunciation to young learners can be easier because they are usually very willing to repeat words and phrases several times. Young learners are also good mimics, so they do not find it difficult to learn to make new sounds and words. Young children like to move around a lot, so you can show them how to make arm movements to illustrate intonation patterns (see page 57). Then they can conduct their intonation practice.

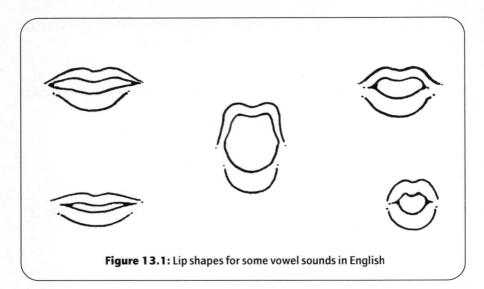

Figure 13.1: Lip shapes for some vowel sounds in English

Teaching pronunciation to adult beginners has different challenges. Older learners are often shy of trying new language in front of other students, so choral repetition can encourage them to join in with the group (see page 68).

Here are some sample recognition activities and production activities to help improve students' pronunciation. The areas of pronunciation we cover are:

▶ sounds;
▶ word stress;
▶ sentence stress;
▶ sounds in connected speech;
▶ intonation.

13.2 SOUNDS

For the following activities it is helpful (but not essential) if you and your students can use the International Phonetic Alphabet (IPA), which has a special symbol for each of the 44 sounds of English. Some dictionaries give an IPA pronunciation for each word and this helps learners pronounce the word correctly.

In this section, we sometimes show the phonetic symbols for sounds to help you understand some points of pronunciation. However, you can teach pronunciation effectively and your students can learn pronunciation without knowing the IPA.

The words in the following activities are based upon the pronunciation of standard British English. You may need to choose other words which have the different sounds used in your local variety of English.

Activities to recognize sounds

105. Minimal sound pairs

Materials: none.

Write a list of pairs of words which sound the same (such as 'peace' and 'piece') and other pairs of words which have one sound different (such as 'peace' and 'peas'). Read all the pairs out loud in random order. Ask students to raise their right hand if they think the sounds are the same, and to raise their left hand if they think the sounds are different.

This exercise can be done with words that have different sounds at the beginning, middle or end of a word.

Some minimal pair types in standard British English:

Initial sound differences: sing/thing, sum/thumb, heel/wheel, vest/west, goat/coat;

Middle sound differences: hat/heart, shut/shirt, work/walk, pot/put, corn/coin;

Final sound differences: thin/think, mouse/mouth, pass/path, tore/toy, watch/wash.

106. Odd one out?

Materials: none.

Write sets of three or four words, one of which does *not* share a sound common to the other words. For example: go/so/do/no (the odd one out is 'do'). Ask students to mark the odd one out in each set. To check their answers, they can read out each set of words on the list to a partner, or take turns in front of the class.

107. Sound bingo

Materials: small cards.

Make a card like the ones shown in Figure 13.2 for each student. If you copy the different cards, every fourth student will have the same card. The words on the cards have a long or a short vowel sound in them. If your students need to practise other sounds, you can write different words on your cards.

Another way to do this activity is to write 20–30 words on the board and ask students to copy eight words from the board onto a card.

Ask the class to listen to each vowel sound you dictate and to decide if any of the words on their card contains this sound. If they do hear a sound which is in one of their words, they cross out the word on their card.

You then dictate, in random order, the vowel sounds the words contain. Remember to say the vowel sound only, not the whole word. This way, students will concentrate on recognizing individual sounds. Note down the order in which you dictated the sounds.

The first student to cross out all the words on their card is the winner. To check, this student can read the words and the rest of the class can agree or disagree with the pronunciation.

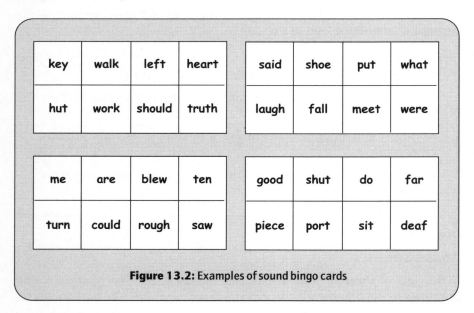

Figure 13.2: Examples of sound bingo cards

108. Sound snap

Materials: small cards.

Make sets of 20–30 cards, each with a word on it which has a different sound. You could use the words with different vowel sounds on the bingo cards above or words with different initial sounds or different final sounds. You can also write words on the board for students to copy to make their own cards.

In groups of between three and six, students divide their pack of cards so that everyone has about the same number of cards. The opening player places one card face up in the middle of the table. Students then take turns in placing one of their cards on the table so that everyone can see the two cards. If the student who placed their card on the table thinks that the words on the two cards contain the same sound, he or she can say 'Snap', and take all the cards on the table. This student then places a new card face up in the middle of the table. The next student then places their card and checks whether they match. If these two cards do not match, then the students continue around the group, each placing a card, until a matching card is found. The winner is the student who has the most cards.

Activities to practise sounds

109. Sound dictation

Materials: the board.

Across the top of the board, write two or three words with different sounds that your students need to practise. Below them, write in random order a list of words. Each word should contain one of the vowel sounds your students need to practise.

For example, to practise the middle vowels, you can choose the vowel sounds in the words heart, hurt and heat. Write those across the top of the board. Underneath, you can then write the following words which have these vowel sounds: cast, feet, bird, wheat, past, start, curl, me.

Students copy the words onto a sheet of paper, placing each word with a different sound in a different column. In pairs, one student is a speaker and the other a writer. The speaker reads out a word on the list, and the writer has to write these words into the column of the word with the same sounds (so, for example, 'cart' goes under 'heart'). Then they change roles and do the activity again, so each student has a chance to speak and to write. The students then compare what they have written.

110. Where's the star?

Materials: the board.

This sample activity gives students practice with some sounds that may confuse language learners. For example, practise the difference between the words for the numbers 13 and 30, 14 and 40 and so on, and the difference between the letters A, E, I, O and U. However, you can include any letters that your students find difficult to understand, pronounce or distinguish between, such as T/D, B/V, G/K or L/R, for example.

Draw the matrix in Figure 13.3 on the board. Then students can either do the activity on the board in teams, or they can copy the matrix onto a sheet of paper and work in pairs.

	A	E	I	O	U
13		*			
14					
16					
17				*	
30					
40			*		
60					
70					

Figure 13.3: Sound recognition matrix

One member of each team, or each student, chooses and writes down the position of three stars in three boxes on their copy of the matrix. For example, 13–E, 40–I, 17–O. The other team, or other student in each pair, asks: 'Is it 13A?' If this is correct, the student asking the question draws a star in that box on their copy of the matrix. If this is not correct, the student continues asking. The winner is the team or student who correctly guesses all the stars' positions first.

13.3 WORD STRESS

Spoken English has sounds and syllables. For example, the word 'dog' has three sounds: d/o/g, but only one syllable. The word 'market' has two syllables (mar/ket) and the word 'photograph' has three syllables: (pho/to/graph). When a word has two or more syllables, one syllable is stressed, which means it is spoken louder and longer. The unstressed syllables are spoken more softly and more quickly.

If language learners hear a good model, most of them will be able to use the correct word stress after they have heard a new word several times and repeated it. Correct word stress is important, because incorrect word stress can be a major cause of misunderstandings. The stress for individual words is best learnt when students first learn the word.

How to help students with word stress

To help your students repeat a new word with the correct stress, ask them to say the word as a series of long 'laa' and short 'la' sounds. So 'dog' becomes 'la', 'market' becomes 'laa la' and 'photograph' becomes 'laa la la'. This technique allows students to concentrate on the stress pattern, without worrying about how to make the correct sounds to pronounce the word at the same time.

You can also demonstrate these stress patterns by clapping or tapping a desk loudly and softly while you say the word. When you write new words on the board, you can help students visualize the stress pattern by writing 'O' for a stressed syllable, and 'o' for an unstressed syllable.

Some stress patterns:

o O	O o	o O o	o o O	O o o	oOoo
machine	doctor	computer	understand	holiday	reliable

Moving word stress

Some two-syllable words change their stress depending on whether they are being used as a verb or as a noun, for example:

o O o   O o

It was recorded in the record book.

Some other words which change their stress in the same way are: increase, decrease, export and import.

Words containing -graph, -scope and -phone have different stress patterns depending on which part of speech they form in a sentence. For example:

O o o

May I photograph you? (verb)

o O o o

My brother is a photographer. (noun)

o o O o

I'd like some photographic paper. (adjective)

Activities to recognize word stress

111. Same or different?

Materials: none.

Make a list of pairs of words that either have the same or different stress patterns. Read out these pairs of words. Ask students to listen carefully and to decide whether these pairs of words have the same or different stress patterns. Students raise their left arm if the patterns are different (for example, holiday/computer), or raise their right arm if the patterns are the same (for example, waiter Oo/cotton Oo).

112. Which stress pattern?

Materials: the board.

Make two lists of words with two different stress patterns. In class, draw only the two different word stress patterns on the board, one on the left-hand side and one on the right-hand side of the board. Then read out the words on your sheet of paper in random order. Students have to distinguish between the two stress patterns in one of two ways:

1. Students copy the stress patterns only and then write each word that you say under the correct stress pattern.

2. Students raise one arm after you have said each word. They raise their left arm when they hear a word which has the same stress as the pattern on the left side on the board, or they raise their right arm when they hear a word which has the same stress as the pattern on the right side of the board.

113. Word stress bingo

Materials: the board.

Write some different stress patterns on the board. Ask students to choose two, three or four of these patterns and to write them down. Then you dictate ten to 15 words that fit the stress patterns on the board. The students must decide if the word you dictate fits one of the stress patterns they have chosen. When they hear a word with one of their stress patterns, they can cross out that pattern on their list. The winner is the student who correctly crosses out all the stress patterns on their list. This activity can also be played as a team competition.

Activities to practise word stress

114. Student word stress bingo

Materials: the board.

Write four to six different stress patterns on the board.

Ask students to choose two to four of these patterns and write them down. The students work in groups. Give one student in each group a list of words which match the stress patterns on the board. This student dictates the words one by one to their group. The other students listen carefully and decide if the pronunciation of each word fits a pattern they have written down. When they hear one of the words, they cross out the stress pattern on their list. The winner is the first student who correctly crosses out all the stress patterns on their list.

115. Word stress charts

Materials: chart paper or the back of a poster.

Make a chart showing some stress patterns and ask students to copy the chart into their notebooks.

As students learn new words during the year, they can write them in the correct column of the chart.

This activity can be made into a team competition, with a chart for each group. The winner is the group which finishes first with all words correctly placed.

13.4 SENTENCE STRESS

Spoken English has a distinctive rhythm. Again, as for word stress, students need to be aware of the importance of using the correct sentence stress. Stressing certain syllables or words in a sentence gives a specific meaning to that sentence, so incorrect sentence stress can cause problems in understanding. These activities show how you use word stress to emphasize new or different information in a sentence.

Activities to recognize sentence stress

116. Stressing what?

Materials: sheets of paper or small cards.

Read out some short sentences, each of which has one word strongly stressed. Ask students to listen and to write down the word which they think is stressed on a piece of paper. After each sentence, ask students to hold up their answers. If any answers are wrong, say the sentence again so they can listen again and get it right.

Variation 1: Place a copy of the stress pattern chart on the wall of the classroom, and as students learn new words they can add them to the correct stress pattern. This produces a resource for the whole class.

Variation 2: Give students a random list of words which they have to write in the correct column of the stress pattern chart within a fixed time limit. This activity can be made into a team competition. Each team works on the same chart and the winner is the group which finishes first with all words correctly placed.

117. Same sentence/different stress

Materials: the board.

Write four identical sentences on the board, number them and underline a different word in each sentence. Then, in random order, say each sentence in a different way, stressing a different word each time. Ask students to guess which sentence you have said, matching it to the written underlined form.

Then write the different meanings of each sentence in a second column but do *not* line up the matching pairs of sentences. Next, ask students to match the different meanings to the different underlined sentences.

Differently stressed sentences	Different meanings
1. I saw *Marta* running outside yesterday.	a. (I usually see Rosa.)
2. I saw Marta *running* outside yesterday.	b. (I usually see Marta walking.)
3. I saw Marta running *outside* yesterday.	c. (Marta usually runs inside.)
4. I saw Marta running outside *yesterday*.	d. (Marta usually runs at the weekend.)

Activities to practise sentence stress

118. Food shopping

Materials: the board and posters.

Divide the class into shopkeepers and customers and get the students to work in pairs: a shopkeeper with a customer. Write two lists on the board, or you can write the lists on two posters and place them on opposite sides of the classroom. The list of what shopkeepers sell could be: plain chocolate, red peppers, white rice, ground coffee and white bread. The customers have a list of what they want to buy, for example: milk chocolate, green peppers, brown rice, instant coffee and brown bread.

The customer asks for the items on their list: 'Do you have any white sugar?'

The shopkeeper replies: 'No sorry, I've only got *brown* sugar', and so on.

119. Job comparisons

Materials: the board.

Make two columns on the board headed 'relatives' and 'jobs'. Ask the students to give examples of relatives and jobs. Students then work in pairs. Student A makes a sentence, using one word from the 'relative' column and one word from the 'jobs' column. Student B then repeats the sentence, but replaces student A's job with another job. Student B has to use correct word stress to indicate the new meaning. Student A then repeats the sentence, this time changing the relative and again using word stress to indicate the new meaning.

Example:

Student A: 'My cousin's a pharmacist.'

Student B: 'My cousin's an *accountant*.'

Student A: 'My *uncle's* an accountant.'

Variation: the correct version.

Materials: the board and small cards.

Write two sets of words on the board, one with five different days of the week, and the other with five different towns which your students know. Ask the students to copy these two sets of words onto a piece of paper. Next, they cut the paper into ten individual cards. In pairs, students place the two sets of cards face down on the table. Student A picks up one card from each set, and from the information on them, makes a sentence.

For example, if the cards say 'Blantyre' and 'Wednesday', Student A says: 'Are you going to Blantyre on Wednesday?'

Student B then picks up a 'day' card and replies: 'No, I'm going to Blantyre on *Friday*'.

Student A picks up a 'town' card and asks: 'When are you going to *Lilongwe*?'

Student B then picks up a 'day' card and says: 'I'm going to Lilongwe on *Tuesday*'.

Student A says something like this: '*I'm* going to Lilongwe on Tuesday too – can I have a lift?'

Student B can finish the conversation in any possible way, then they change roles and pick up different cards and have a similar conversation.

120. Where were you?

Materials: the board.

Student A:	'<u>Where</u> were you last night?'
Student B:	' I was <u>out</u>.'
Student A:	'<u>Who</u> were you with?'
Student B:	'I was with my <u>friends</u>.'
Student A:	'<u>Where</u> did you go?'
Student B:	'We went to the <u>park</u>.'
Student A:	'<u>What</u> did you do?'
Student B:	'We played <u>football</u>.'

Write this dialogue on the board. Model each line, making sure you stress each underlined word strongly. Ask students to repeat each line several times. Then students say this dialogue in pairs, using either four, six or eight of the lines.

Variation: to practise a more challenging dialogue, students have to choose their own answers for line 4 (for example, change 'friends' to 'brothers'), line 6 (for example, change 'park' to 'cinema') and line 8 (for example, change 'played football' to 'watched a film').

13.5 SOUNDS IN CONNECTED SPEECH

English has a distinctive rhythm with a steady beat, so the time between all stressed syllables is approximately the same. To keep this beat regular, the small words and the less important words must become weak or unstressed.

For example, the following three sentences can be spoken in the same length of time.

beat 1		beat 2		beat 3		beat 4
YOU	and	ME	and	HIM	and	HER.
YOU	and then	ME	and then	HIM	and then	HER.
YOU and then it's		ME and then it's		HIM and then it's		HER.

In this example, the syllables in lower case letters have all been squeezed into the same beat. Weak sounds and contracted words (or contractions) are the main features of connected speech.

Some common contractions

wasn't / weren't / you'd / you'll / you've / I'll / I've / I'm / I'd / they'll / they're / they've / they'd / she'll / he'll / she'd / he'd / wouldn't / shouldn't / couldn't / doesn't / don't / won't / haven't / hasn't / hadn't / must've / mustn't / may've / might've/ can't / it's / isn't / it'll / aren't / who's / where's / when's / how's / why's

Some common words that have weak forms

A / an / and / are / at / but / can / could / do / does / for / from / her / had / has / of / shall / should / some / than / that / the / them / to / was / were

Some common words that have weak forms:

a / ə /; an / ən /; and / ənd /; are / ə /; at / ət/; but / bət /; can / ƙən /; could / ƙəd /; do / də /; does / dəz /; for / fə /; from / frəm /; her / hə /; had / həd /; has / həz /; of / əv /; shall / ʃəl /; should / ʃəd /; some / səm /; than / ðən /; that / ðət /; the / ðə /; them / ðəm /; to / tə /; was / wəz /; were / wə

The weak forms of these words have the 'shuwa' vowel sound.

Figure 13.4: Phonetic translation of some weak forms of words

Here is an example to contrast the weak and strong form of 'I am':

Student A: 'What are you doing?'

Student B: 'I'm <u>reading</u>.'

Student A: 'Read <u>faster</u>.'

Student B: 'I <u>am</u> reading fast.'

Student A: What are you doing?

Student B: I'm / aɪm / **reading.**

Student A: Read **faster.**

Student B: I **am** / aɪ æm / reading fast.

Figure 13.5: Phonetic translation of a dialogue with 'I am'

Activity to recognize sounds in connected speech

121. What am I saying?

Materials: none.

In normal speech, some small and less important words contract (shorten) to fit the regular beat of an English sentence. Write down some sentences with different contractions. Say these sentences and ask students to find the full forms of the words you contracted.

For example:

▶   They'll come when they're ready. = They will . . . they are . . .
▶   He'd been asking if they'd played well. = He had . . . they had . . .

Students repeat your contracted sentences. Then they can make up their own sentences and dialogues that include different contractions. In pairs, students take turns in saying and repeating each other's sentences in contracted and full forms.

Activities to practise sounds in connected speech

122. You, me, him, her

Materials: none.

Model each line and ask students to repeat each line individually. Help them to keep the beat by tapping gently on the desk or beating your arm in the air as you speak. Do this several times and when they can repeat each line easily and quickly, ask students to say all three lines with you. Continue to keep the beat for them.

beat 1		beat 2		beat 3		beat 4
YOU	and	ME	and	HIM	and	HER.
YOU	and then	ME	and then	HIM	and then	HER.
YOU	and then it's	ME	and then it's	HIM	and then it's	HER.

Figure 13.6: Strong beats and sentence stress

123. Nursery rhymes

Materials: the board.

A more exciting and challenging way to practise keeping the beat and squeezing words and sounds together is to say a children's rhyme with young pupils. You and your young learners probably know many traditional children's rhymes which you can use in the classroom.

Variation: for older students or adult learners, you can use jazz chants. Jazz chants are like poems: they have rhyming sounds at the end of some lines and a strong rhythm.

Here is an example of a jazz chant:

'What next?
What're you gonna do when you finish this course?'
'I might run a restaurant or I might write a book
I might be a tailor or I might learn to cook
I might go to med. school or I might study law
Or I might get married, I'm not really sure.'

Dictate the jazz chant, or ask students to copy it from the board. First, model the jazz chant line by line. Then ask students to repeat each line after you. Next, divide the class into two and ask each half to read alternate lines. Then divide the class into pairs and ask all the class to read alternate lines (quietly!). Help students keep the beat by gently tapping on the desk or by marking the beat in the air with your arm.

124. Shadow reading

Materials: the board.

Find or write a short text which can be read in about 20–30 seconds. It is a good idea to record it on tape because this helps to ensure the same pronunciation every time students hear it. If you do not have a tape recorder, read the text to the class. Pause at the end of each sentence for the students to repeat. Encourage them to repeat fairly quickly to help them say the weak forms of English naturally.

13.6 INTONATION

Some basic intonation patterns

Intonation is the music of a language, meaning how our voice rises and falls at certain points of the sentence. Different English intonation patterns can change the meaning of a sentence. So students need to be aware of the meanings of different patterns and also need to be able to say the different patterns appropriately. The main intonation patterns in standard British English are a rising tone or a falling tone.

A rising tone is used:

▶ to ask questions that are answered with 'yes' or 'no', for example:
- Are you ready?
- Do you want to go out?
- You're Russian, aren't you?

▶ to express emotions, such as interest, shock, or surprise, for example:
- Really!
- What!
- Would you like to win one thousand pounds? Yes!

A falling tone is used:

► to ask questions beginning with what/when/where/who/which/
why/how, for example:
* When shall we go?
* How much is this please?

► to say statements, for example:
* I like bananas.
* Let's go shopping.

To help students hear the intonation, you can show the rise and fall of the
sentence by arm and hand movements as you speak. Remember that the
students are sitting opposite you, so you have to move your arm from right
to left! Also you can illustrate intonation by writing a sentence on the board
and drawing a rising or falling arrow over it as appropriate.

Activity to recognize intonation patterns

125. What can you hear?

Materials: the board.

Make a list of words or sentences. Draw only the intonation patterns
of these sentences on the board, either with a rising or falling pattern.
Read these sentences aloud, with appropriate intonation. Ask the students
to decide whether the intonation goes up or down. They can either draw
the correct pattern in their notebooks or take turns making a tick under the
correct pattern on the board.

Activities to practise intonation patterns

126. Lists

Materials: the board.

Going around the class (or students can work in groups), each student in
turn adds to a list, for example:

► something they want to buy;
► places they have visited;
► films they have seen;
► food they like.

The first student, A, starts the list by saying, for example: 'I went shopping and I bought a newspaper'.

The next student repeats the list, adding an item of their own choice: 'I went shopping and I bought a newspaper and an ice cream'.

Other students repeat the full list and each adds their own item.

Remember that the intonation goes down on the last item, as it is new information. To make the list easier to remember, you or a student can write each item on the board.

127. Say it differently

Materials: none.

The following four-line dialogue can be said in different ways. It could be said happily, sadly, angrily or politely. Students repeat after you.

Student A: 'May I borrow your pen?'

Student B: 'No, I'm sorry you can't.'

Student A: 'Oh, it doesn't matter.'

Student B: 'But I can lend you a pencil.'

Next, half of the class takes the part of Student A, and the other half of the class takes the part of Student B. Students in pairs can say the dialogue happily, sadly, angrily or politely. For a change, they can alternate moods, so Student A can act happy or polite, while Student B can act sad or angry.

128. Storytelling

Materials: none.

This activity helps students to listen to a story and to retell it with interesting and dramatic intonation. The story can either be a well-known traditional story or one that you and the students create. You start to tell the story, but in a monotonous voice. Stop after one or two sentences.

Invite a student, A, to retell your part of the story, but putting drama and emotion into the words. Then, Student A continues with the next bit of the story, but in a monotonous tone of voice. The next student, B, retells your and Student A's story with a range of intonation to give it interest, but adds their own part in a monotonous voice. This continues until someone finishes the story or until everyone has had an opportunity to contribute.

In this section, we have shown a variety of ways to help students recognize and practise English pronunciation. We have used resources, student–teacher interactions and teaching and learning techniques which easily bring variety into your classroom. This variety can help interest and motivate students and can make an activity easier or more challenging, as well as allowing you to vary the length of time it takes.

14/ Testing Speaking Skills

In this section, we look at different kinds of speaking tests and suggest some basic guidelines for devising a good speaking test. Speaking tests can take up a lot of classroom time, so there are some tips for dealing with the practical side of organizing them. We consider what areas you can test and help you to draw up some criteria for testing. We also examine ways of marking. We give many sample activities in each of these areas. They are suggestions to guide you but you can develop your own questions which are suitable for your students and your course.

14.1 TYPES OF TESTS

It is very important to know *why* you want to test your students' speaking so that you can decide what kind of test to give them. Let's look at four different kinds of tests:

- ▶ achievement tests;
- ▶ placement tests;
- ▶ diagnostic tests;
- ▶ proficiency tests.

Achievement tests

Achievement tests are the most common type of test. They are sometimes called progress or attainment tests. They are used to find out what students have learnt. These tests must therefore be based on the content and language of the syllabus or the course book you have been using. You can do achievement tests at the end of every month, every term or every year.

If test results are disappointing, maybe you need to think about the teaching methods you use, or whether new material is being introduced too quickly. Maybe the test is just too difficult, so keep your expectations of your students realistic. Success motivates students, so a realistic achievement test is important.

Placement tests

Placement tests enable us to sort students into groups of similar and appropriate levels. Such tests have to be as general as possible and cover a wide range of abilities. A placement test anticipates the language demands which will be expected of students, so it is important to link the test closely to the syllabus which students will follow.

Diagnostic tests

Diagnostic tests are often done at the beginning of a course. They enable us to find out the exact needs of your students so that you can plan the syllabus or learning programme.

Proficiency tests

Proficiency tests are often set by outside institutes. They test the students' ability to use English in real-life communication.

Guidelines for setting up a good test

Here are some guidelines to help you set a valid and fair test.

▶ Give students lots of practice in doing speaking tests before the real test or examination.

▶ Make sure that the instructions are very clear and simple. Students should understand exactly what they are expected to do.

▶ Devise a simple marking system that is easy for other examiners to follow. This helps to ensure that examiners mark consistently.

▶ Make sure that all examiners understand the marking system. This removes possible bias and maximizes the chance that a student would get the same mark whoever tested him/her. If possible, have a meeting before the real test, or give examiners a chance to be interlocutor (see below) before being responsible for giving marks.

▶ Decide on a reasonable pass mark. A test which is so difficult that most students fail is not helpful because it does not give you useful information about what they have learned. And remember: success motivates students.

▶ Make sure students know exactly which areas they are being tested on and how many marks are given for different aspects of speaking, for example, accurate use of tenses, a wide range of vocabulary or a good awareness of levels of formality.

14.2 ORGANIZING SPEAKING TESTS

Testing students' speaking ability individually can take up a lot of classroom time, particularly in large classes. Here are some ideas to help you:

▶ Test students in pairs or in groups of three. Be careful how you group students to avoid stronger students dominating weaker ones. Girls may like to be grouped with girls and boys with boys.

▶ Give the class a writing activity and while whey are doing this, call out individuals, pairs or groups to another room to test them where they cannot disturb the writers.

▶ Avoid writing marks while students are speaking as this can disturb their concentration. Write down the marks immediately after the test. Otherwise, it is easy to forget what level a student actually achieved. If possible, record the speaking test on a tape recorder.

▶ Recording speaking tests in a language laboratory with several tape recorders is a very efficient way of testing many students at the same time because several students can record their tests onto different tapes simultaneously.

▶ If, as examiner, you are the only other person in the conversation, make sure that you prompt or question all students in a similar way. What you say can very easily influence a student's performance, so you need to make sure you are testing them all in the same way.

▶ It is difficult to take part in a conversation and assess a student's performance at the same time. If possible, ask another English teacher to act as *interlocutor*. This means that the other teacher speaks to the student, so that you can concentrate on listening and giving marks.

▶ If it is possible to video some examinations, these can be used to standardize marking schemes and to help train new examiners.

▶ If necessary, test students over several lessons.

▶ Put the students at their ease when they come in so that they relax and can perform at their best. Speak in a friendly way and ask a few easy questions first, like 'What is your name?', 'Have I written that correctly?', 'How old are you?', and so on.

14.3 WHAT KIND OF LANGUAGE DO WE TEST?

In any of the four kinds of test, we may want to find out about distinct language areas, such as:

▶ pronunciation;
▶ grammatical accuracy;

► range of vocabulary;
► use of appropriate functional language.

Other skills you might want to test are:

► adequacy of vocabulary for purpose;
► intelligibility;
► fluency ;
► appropriateness of functional language;
► relevance and adequacy of content.

We can focus on these areas by making a suitable marking scheme but the test itself should be as near as possible to a real-life situation using real-life language. A real-life situation involves two kinds of oral performance: informing and interacting.

Informing

When we want to test students' ability to inform, we can ask them to:

► describe something;
► compare two or three things;
► give instructions about how to do something;
► tell a story;
► use a longer piece of narrative to tell about some event or how something works.

These oral skills are particularly useful for testing students individually, even those at an elementary level. Pictures or a series of pictures, diagrams, maps, leaflets, posters or student notes can all be used as prompts to test this kind of language skill.

Interacting

Testing students' ability to interact can, of course, only be done in pairs or groups, although sometimes the examiner may have to take the other role in the conversation. Pairs, groups or student and examiner can perform speaking activities such as:

► buying and selling;
► comparing information;
► interviewing each other;
► attending meetings or making decisions.

Once again, pictures, objects, timetables, diaries, agenda and situations can be used to prompt the discussion.

Testing the social skills of communication

You might need to test how well students can use the social skills of communication. For example:

▶ what do they do if they don't understand another speaker?
▶ can they ask for clarification?
▶ do they know how to break into a conversation?

They may also have to:

▶ know the cultural norms of taking turns in a conversation;
▶ know how to use language at the correct level of formality (for advanced students).

14.4 ASSESSING AND MARKING

We have looked at a very wide range of language and oral skills which you can test. However, since you may only be able to give each student or group five or ten minutes for their test, you have to ask yourself what skills you wish to give marks for. Once you have decided this, you can devise a very simple marking scheme. Here are two ways of doing this.

Marking scheme for separate language areas

Let us assume that you want to set a speaking achievement test to assess the accuracy of students' use of language they have learned. The chart opposite (Figure 14.1) will help you produce a fairly consistent set of marks.

In most charts like this, it is preferable to use an even number of levels (for example, we used four levels in Figure 14.1: poor, fair, good, excellent). If you use odd numbers, such as three or five, it is tempting to compromise on the middle mark, for example, a three out of five, rather than thinking hard about the performance.

If several examiners are using the same marking scheme, there needs to be an accompanying document which says what is meant by poor, fair, good, excellent (see below).

Rating scales

It is very common now to use a system of ratings which judge the overall effectiveness of the message, rather than criteria which divide the language

	Excellent	Good	Fair	Poor
Vocabulary (Accuracy, range)				
Grammar (Sentence construction, use of tenses)				
Functions (Accuracy, appropriateness)				

Figure 14.1: A marking scheme for language areas

into separate areas. Rating scales can be used for placement, diagnostic and proficiency tests. However, they may not be specific enough for achievement tests.

Rating	Ability to communicate orally
6	Excellent. Completely at ease in use of English on all topics discussed. Very good communication skills.
5	Very good. No difficulty in understanding English and there are no problems communicating with the student. Good strategies for keeping the conversation flowing.
4	Student makes a limited number of errors of grammar, vocabulary and pronunciation, but is still at ease in communicating on everyday subjects. Knows his/her own mistakes and can correct him/herself.
3	Occasional difficulties in communicating. Several errors which sometimes make it difficult to communicate with the student.
2	Student's understanding is severely limited, but communication on everyday topics is possible. A large number of errors.
1	Cannot understand adequately and cannot make him/herself understood.

Figure 14.2: An example of a marking sheet that uses rating scales

When you are trying to decide on a mark, first think quickly roughly which levels the student might be in: the top two, the middle two or the bottom two. After that, become more specific and decide which of the two levels is more appropriate.

Continuous assessment

Continuous assessment is a way of monitoring the progress of students during the year. It is usually used in addition to other tests. It is a useful way to assess students because:

▶ it helps teachers and students to identify their strengths and weaknesses as they learn;

▶ it indicates which areas students must work on before the end-of-term test or the examination;

▶ some aspects of students' performance are not easy to measure in tests, for example, participation, attitude and co-operation in group tasks;

▶ there are students who become so nervous in examinations that they do not perform at their expected standard.

Continuous assessment is part of a supportive learning atmosphere. While students are doing usual classroom activities, walk round quietly and make notes on cards or in a small notebook. Don't make it obvious that you are assessing the students and restrict your observation to six or seven students in each lesson. Be sure that you know the names of students.

At the start of the course, you can tell your students that you will do this. You can also tell them that you will give them a mark every week or two weeks, but that their worst two or three marks will be discarded. After a while, they will forget that you are assessing them during lessons.

When you know which areas are weak for all or some students, you can revise these areas. Do not name individual students but you can introduce the review by saying, 'Some of you need a bit more help with . . .' or, 'I think we need to look at . . . again.'

14.5 IDEAS FOR TESTING SPOKEN ENGLISH

Here are some test formats with suggestions for what the examiner might say to the candidate.

Testing students' ability to hear and repeat

Copying sounds

Instructions: ask the students to listen to you (the examiner) or a tape, and to repeat exactly what you say. The sentences should include sounds that students find difficult. The sentences should become longer and more complex.

This tests: ability to hear sounds and to copy sounds, intonation, stress and linking patterns.

Testing the ability to give information

Talking about a picture

Instructions: give the student a picture and ask him/her to describe what he/she can see. Then, ask his/her opinion about things in the picture. For example:

► Tell me what you can see in this picture.
► What do you think has just happened?
► What do you think will happen next?
► Have you had an experience like this?
► How would you feel if you were this person?

This tests: range and accuracy of vocabulary, using the correct form and use of grammatical structures (present continuous, future, past tenses, conditionals), appropriate ways of expressing opinions.

Variation: at a lower level and for young learners, you can ask students simple questions like:

► What colour is this?
► How many apples are there?
► What is this? (point to an object)
► Where is the bicycle?

Talking about an object

Instructions: bring a box of small interesting objects to the examination or ask students to bring an object from home which they find interesting. If the examiner brings the objects give students five minutes before the examination to prepare a mini-presentation about the object. You can encourage them by asking questions such as:

► Tell me about this object.
► Where did you get it from?
► Why did you choose it?
► How does it work?

This tests: range and accuracy of vocabulary, passive constructions (it's made of . . . , it's used for . . . , it was given to me by . . .), comparatives, adjectives, expressing likes and dislikes, describing how things work.

Describing a series of events

Instructions: give the student a series of small pictures which show a sequence of events and ask him/her to tell the story in the past tense. Give students some time to prepare this (ten minutes should be enough).

This tests: range and accuracy of vocabulary, form and use of grammatical structures.

Testing the ability to interact with other speakers

Responses

Instructions: tell the student that you will say a short phrase (or they will hear it on the tape), for example,

▶   Can I borrow your pen?
▶   It's really cold in here.

They have to respond with one or two sentences. This test is usually done individually.

This tests: accuracy of functional language and appropriateness of response.

Mini-situations

Instructions: tell the student that you will tell them about a situation, and they have to say the exact words they would use if they were in this situation. For example, the student has to say, 'Can I borrow your umbrella?', not 'I would ask him if I could borrow his umbrella'.

Example situations:

▶   You are on the platform of a station. You want to know if you are on the correct platform for your train. What do you say to someone standing near you?
▶   You are late for a football practice. What do you say to the teacher when you arrive?

This tests: accuracy and appropriateness of functional language.

Information gap activity

Instructions: students work in pairs. Each has a document with different information. They have to exchange information and come to a conclusion.

Examples:

► The students each have information about different colleges. They have to compare them and decide which is the better college to apply to.
► One student has a map and the other has information about where he/she is and where he/she wants to go. They have to discuss the best way to get there.

This tests: range and accuracy of vocabulary, form and use of grammatical-structures, functional language of putting forward an opinion and agreeing or disagreeing, social communication skills.

Dialogues

Instructions: students work in pairs as A and B. Give them a realistic situation which could happen in their lives and ask them to hold a dialogue. When you have given students the topic, let them prepare what they want to ask or say for a few minutes.

Example topics:

► Ranju has just met an interesting new friend. Jafor asks questions to find out about the person.
► Julia is an English student staying with Merciline in her country. Merciline is studying English. Merciline asks Julia about how birthdays are celebrated in Britain. Julia and Merciline compare the different traditions of gifts, food, activities, etc.

This tests: accuracy and range of vocabulary, form and use of grammatical structures, social communication skills, factual knowledge which has been taught during the course (for example, knowledge about festivals in other countries).

Structured interview

Instructions: hold an interview with the student based on a series of questions which prompt various language skills (for example, use of tenses).

Example questions:

► When is your birthday?
► How many brothers and sisters do you have?
► What are you going to do after school/college/work today?
► What did you do last Sunday?
► Where have you travelled within your country?
► Have you ever been to another country?
► What country would you like to go to?
► What do you want to do when you finish your studies?

This tests: use and appropriateness of functional language, accuracy and range of vocabulary, form and use of grammatical structures, social skills of communication.

15 / Summary and Ways Forward

15.1 SUMMARY

In this book, we have given you a selection of tried and tested teaching ideas to help you improve your students' speaking skills. We hope the ideas will encourage you to try new teaching and learning techniques.

Remember that the first time you try a new idea or technique, it may not work out as well as you expected. This is normal, but if you try some more activities, you will find that you quickly become better at planning and managing activities.

To help you do activities successfully, check whether you need to:

► explain the activity more simply;
► reinforce explanations by writing them on the board;
► demonstrate the activity with strong students;
► organize pairs and groups quickly;
► monitor the students, by looking and listening carefully.

Keep trying new teaching and learning techniques and ideas. Remember that it takes a bit of time for you and your students to feel comfortable doing different kinds of activities, but that they will help your students learn better and become better speakers of English.

15.2 WAYS FORWARD

Both of us have taught English and trained teachers in several different countries, and this book includes activities we used and saw in our work. We have also included ideas from VSO and national teachers of English worldwide. However, each school has a unique situation and you may face unique challenges that we have not covered. You are the best person to decide what your students need.

This book suggests many different ideas and techniques. We would like you to take the ideas in this book and move forward with them. We hope we have given you enough explanation and support to do this. We also hope you will continue to expand and enjoy your teaching in ways that are appropriate for your students in your individual context.

Index of Activities

ACTIVITY	DESCRIPTION
Warmers	
1 Favourites	Talking about favourite activities, people or objects
2 Me too!	Finding things in common
3 That's nice!	Saying what you like about other people
4 My life	Telling about your recent activities
5 Word collecting	Collecting words on given topics
6 Definitions	Match definitions to words
Variation	Give words and ask for definitions
7 Same or different	Finding synonyms and antonyms
8 Word groups	Organizing random words into categories
Variation	Organizing verbs into different categories
9 Scales	Putting words in order according to meaning
10 Prefixes	Finding words which take certain prefixes
11 Word hunt	Making short words from long ones
12 Team sentences	Making long sentences in teams
13 Touch the box	Racing to identify new vocabulary
14 Guess the word	Making and matching definitions of new vocabulary
15 Learning names	Learning students' names
16 I went to market	Remembering new vocabulary
17 Alphabet chains	Using the alphabet to remember vocabulary
Variation	Omit difficult letters of the alphabet
18 Crosswords	Crosswords based on new vocabulary
Variation	Students make own crosswords
19 Word search	Spotting vocabulary hidden in a puzzle
20 Mystery boxes	Asking the teacher questions
21 Topic circle	Brief conversations on interesting topics
22 Alphabet circle	Learning about classmates and their names

23	Mystery lines	Trying to find out another team's secret information
24	Shark attack	A way of scoring team activities
	Variation	More positive version with prize
25	Noughts and crosses	A way of testing and scoring team activities

Controlled practice

26	Repetition drills	Practising vocabulary, grammar and functions for accuracy
	Variation 1	Practising vocabulary with objects belonging to students
	Variation 2	Practising drilling with nominated students
27	Substitution drills	Bringing some variety into repetition drills
	Variation	Drilling with charts
28	Information gap drills	Finding information from other students
	Variation 1	Finding more detailed information from other students
	Variation 2	Finding information working in pairs
29	Questionnaires	Finding and recording information from other students
	Variation	Finding and recording information about more sophisticated topics from other students
30	Disappearing dialogues	Techniques for remembering dialogues
31	Kim's game	A memory activity using real objects or pictures
32	Guessing activities	Asking questions to guess what others are thinking
	Variation 1	Asking questions using more difficult language
	Variation 2	Asking questions about hidden objects
	Variation 3	Asking questions about famous people

Less controlled activities

33	Practising use of tenses	Using cards to check correct use of tenses
34	Filling in forms	Role playing real-life situations in hotels, offices, etc.
35	Information gap diaries	Comparing and discussing plans and appointments
36	Ordering words to make a correct sentence	Actively building very long sentences

Practising functional language

37 Inviting and refusing   Using flash cards to practise inviting and refusing
38 Persuading and refusing   Trying not to sell your favourite object
39 Requesting   Collecting objects through requesting
40 Agreeing and disagreeing Discussing topics using prompt cards
41 Keeping going and interrupting   Team activity to practise these functions
42 Tell me more   Conversational strategies and showing interest
43 Conversation chains   Guiding conversations with given prompts
44 Mixed functions   Practising a variety of functions in groups
45 Practising the correct level of formality   Diagnosing and practising functions at the appropriate level
    Variation 1   Role-playing at the appropriate level
    Variation 2   Asking people to perform more demanding tasks

Fluency practice

46 Favourites   Talking about favourite foods, books, films, places
    Variation   Talking about sports and games
47 Characteristics   Asking about people's characteristics
    Variation   Asking about people's habits
48 The whole story   Putting a mixed-up story into a logical order and then retelling it
49 General knowledge   Making questions then answering other students' questions
50 What happens next?   Predicting the end of a story, using a text
    Variation   Predicting the end of a story, using a picture story
51 Thinking differently   Modifying statements about family or community beliefs
    Variation   Ranking a list of values of common interest
52 Making connections   Putting a series of pictures in the right order to tell a story
53 Describe and draw   Describing a picture which students draw
54 Holiday choice   Selecting a holiday from a list of possible holidays
    Variation   Selecting an imaginary holiday destination

55	My favourite animal	Poster presentation of animals using pictures and words
	Variation	Poster presentation of village/town/city using pictures and words
56	A class trip	Planning a class trip
	Variation	Planning an English club
57	The park	Designing a park and making a model of it
	Variation	Designing an ideal school/home/sports ground/garden and making a model of it
58	Public speaking	Presenting a topic with the help of notes
	Variation	Talking to a small group
59	Discussion	Group discussion, with or without reporting back
60	Book review	Group discussion with or without reporting back
	Variation	Group discussion about a film/play with or without reporting back
61	Four chairs	A car/bus/job interview/restaurant/cinema for a role play
	Variation	Acting out one of the above situations to the class
62	The interview	Acting out a job interview
	Variation	Choosing a famous person and acting out an interview with them
63	Factories and farmers	A farmer and a factory owner discussing their different needs
64	Reporter	Making an interview about a newspaper/TV/radio story
	Variation	Acting out a story from a TV/radio/newspaper

Activities based on a narrative text

65	Word collecting	Finding types of words in a text
66	Prediction	Predicting the content of a text from its title
67	Pre-teaching essential vocabulary	Pre-teaching new vocabulary for a text
68	Listening or reading	Listening or reading a text to understand content
69	'Yes'/'No' questions	Testing students' understanding of a text
70	Open questions	Asking open questions about the content of a text
71	Grammatical analysis	Using sentences from the text to teach grammar

72	Grammar	Finding all the examples of a grammatical structure in a text (past continuous with past simple)
73	Grammar	Finding all examples of a grammatical structure in a text (verb + preposition and phrasal verbs)
74	Vocabulary	Finding particular types of words (words which describe motion)
75	Vocabulary	Finding particular types of words (words with prefixes under- and over-)
76	Vocabulary	Finding particular types of words (words which express emotions)
77	Retelling the story	Using a flow chart of verbs to retell the story in students' own words
78	Fluency – role play	Role playing a reporter interviewing characters in the text
79	Production–writing	Writing an article based on the role play in Activity 78
80	Personalization	Preparing a short talk on a given topic
81	Interviews	Interviewing a character in the text
82	Ordering	Putting the story in the right order

Activities based on a factual text

83	Word search	Finding types of words in a puzzle (school subjects)
84	Word collecting	Thinking of as many school subjects as possible
85	Prediction	Predicting the content of a text from a picture
86	Personalization	Students writing down the subjects they study and ranking them
87	Pre-teach essential vocabulary	Pre-teaching new vocabulary for a text
88	Reading for sense and discussion	Reading a text to understand content and discuss difficulties
89	Language work	Finding particular types of words (adverbs)
90	Functional language: preparation for role play	Preparing for role play by learning appropriate functional language (express opinions, agree/disagree)
91	Production – role play	Role playing using functional language of agreeing and disagreeing, expressing opinions

92   Fluency – formal debate   Students debating a topic related to the text
93   Finding a title   Giving the text an appropriate title

Activities based on a dialogue

94   Prediction   Predicting the content of the dialogue from the title
95   Discussion   Discussing controversial issues arising from the dialogue
96   Language work   Finding specific grammatical structures/ synonyms and antonyms
97   Learning the dialogue   Learning the dialogue from memory
98   Discussion and role play   Students speaking about the characters and creating another scene with the same characters

Activities based on poems

99   Gap fill   Filling gaps in the poem and predicting its content
100 Speaking about the poem   Discussing the content of the poem to check understanding then opening discussion to wider topics
101 Language work   Finding specific grammatical structures (adjectives)
102 Brief comparison of the two poems   Answering questions comparing two poems
103 Language work and discussion   Finding specific grammatical structures and types of words
104 Personal response to the poems   Discussing students' reaction to the poems

Pronunciation

105 Minimal sound pairs   Distinguishing between two similar sounds
106 Odd one out?   Choosing the one different sound in a set of sounds
107 Sound bingo   Recognizing sounds quickly
108 Sound snap   Recognizing sounds in different words
109 Sound dictation   Recognizing words containing the same sounds

110	Where's the star?	Saying sounds correctly to identify a matrix reference
111	Same or different?	Recognizing whether two words have the same stress pattern or not
112	Which stress pattern?	Recognizing the stress pattern of different words
113	Word stress bingo	Quickly recognizing word stress patterns
114	Student word stress bingo	Saying words correctly and recognizing these patterns
115	Word stress charts	Filling in charts with words that have the same stress pattern
116	Stressing what?	Recognizing the stressed word in a sentence
	Variation 1	Building a stress pattern chart
	Variation 2	Entering words on a stress pattern chart competition
117	Same sentence/ different stress	Recognizing how a sentence can be stressed differently
118	Food shopping	Stressing sentences to emphasize different information
119	Job comparisons	Stressing sentences to emphasize different information
120	Where were you?	Dialogue with stressed *wh-* questions
	Variation	Using same dialogue students produce some of their own replies
121	What am I saying?	Finding the full forms in contracted sentences
122	You, me, him, her	Expanding sentence said with a strong beat
123	Nursery rhymes	Speaking nursery rhymes fluently with a strong beat
	Variation	Speaking jazz chants fluently with a strong beat
124	Shadow reading	Reading aloud and repeating text
125	What can you hear?	Listening to a sentence and recognizing the intonation pattern
126	Lists	Saying ever-longer lists of items with a final falling intonation
127	Say it differently	Saying a dialogue happily, sadly, angrily or politely
128	Storytelling	Retelling a story with dramatic intonation

VSO Books

VSO Books publishes practical books and Working Papers in education and development based upon the wide range of professional experience of volunteers and their national partners. Practical Working Papers for teachers and development workers are published on VSO's website for free downloading: http://www.vso.org.uk/workingpapers

By the same authors:

The English Language Teacher's Handbook, Joanna Baker and Heather Westrup, VSO/Continuum, 174pp, ISBN 0 8264 4787 2

Books for teachers

The Agricultural Science Teachers' Handbook, Peter Taylor, VSO Books, 148pp, ISBN 0 9509 0507 0

A Handbook for Teaching Sports, National Coaching Foundation, VSO/Heinemann, 160pp, ISBN 0 4359 2320 X

How to Make and Use Visual Aids, Nicola Harford and Nicola Baird, VSO/Heinemann, 128pp, ISBN 0 4359 2317 X

Introductory Technology – A resource book, Adrian Owens, VSO/ITP, 142pp, ISBN 1 8533 9064 X

Life Skills – A training manual for working with street children, Clare Hanbury, VSO/Macmillan, 176pp, ISBN 0 3339 5841 1

The Maths Teachers' Handbook, Jane Portman and Jeremy Richardson, VSO/Heinemann, 108pp, ISBN 0 4359 2318 8

The Science Teachers' Handbook, Andy Byers, Ann Childs, Chris Lainé, VSO/Heinemann, 144pp, ISBN 0 4359 2302 1

Setting Up and Running a School Library, Nicola Baird, VSO/Heinemann, 144pp, ISBN 0 4352 304 8 4

Books for development workers

Adult Literacy – A handbook for development workers, Paul Fordham, Deryn Holland, Juliet Millican, VSO/Oxfam Publications, 192pp, ISBN 0 8559 8315 9

Care and Safe Use of Hospital Equipment, Muriel Skeet and David Fear, VSO Books, 188pp, ISBN 0 9509 0505 4

Diagnosis and Treatment – A training manual for primary health care workers, Dr K. Birrell and Dr G. Birrell, VSO/Macmillan, 272pp, ISBN 0 3337 2211 6.

How to Grow a Balanced Diet, Ann Burgess, Grace Maina, Philip Harris, Stephanie Harris, VSO Books, 244pp, ISBN 0 9509 0506 2

Managing for a Change – How to run community development projects, Anthony Davies, ITP, 160pp, ISBN 1 8533 9339 1

Available soon:

How to Design a Training Course – A guide to participatory curriculum development, Peter Taylor, VSO/Continuum, Spring 2003.

To order or request information about books and discounts, contact:

VSO Books, 317 Putney Bridge Road, London SW15 2PN, UK
Tel: +44 20 8780 7200
Fax: +44 20 8780 7300
E-mail: vsobooks@vso.org.uk
www.vso.org.uk/vsobooks

VSO is an international development agency that promotes volunteering to fight global poverty and disadvantage.

VSO is a registered charity no. 313757.

Index

accuracy 7–8, 24, 34, 89
achievement tests 144
activities 6, 157–63
  based on dialogue 117–19, 161–2
  based on factual text 114–17, 161
  based on narrative text 109–14, 160–1
  based on poems 120–3, 162
  controlled Practice stage 19, 71–7,
    81–2, 158
  and fluency practice 93–106, 159–60
  functional language 59, 81–9, 159
  guided stage 77–81, 82–9, 158–9
  and intonation patterns 141–3
  and motivation 8–9, 16–17
  planning of 22–3
  and pronunciation 127–30, 132–3,
    134–6, 138–40, 141–3, 162–3
  sentence stress practice 134–6
  sentence stress recognition 133–4
  and sounds in connected speech 138–40
  and sounds practice 129–30
  and sounds recognition 127–9
  successful 155
  variations within 31
  warmers 46–55, 110, 116, 118, 157–8
  word stress practice 133
  word stress recognition 132
  writing 95
adult learners 9, 126
assessing 148–50
  continuous 150
attainment tests 144

back chaining 70
barriers to communication 12–17
  cultural differences 12–13
  information overload 15
  lack of confidence 14–15
  lack of interest 16–17
  personal differences 13–14
  and preparation 16
  time problems 15–16

board (blackboard) 40, 51–3
board game 41

cards
  flash cards 41, 42, 69, 71
  for sound bingo 127–8
  for sound snap 128–9
charts
  flow charts 112
  and substitution drills 72
choral drilling 68–70, 89
clarification 91–2
classroom interaction pattern 69
classroom organization 24–33
  group work responsibilities 29–30,
    37
  and helpful phrases 31, 33
  and interactive patterns 26–30, 32
  lesson planning 25
  and noise 30–1
  routines and signals 25–6
  teacher's role 24–5
  variation in activities 24, 31
  see also lesson organization
collocations 60
communication, barriers to *see* barriers to
    communication
communication skills testing 148
confidence and lack of 13–14, 91, 92
  dealing with 14–15
context of language 57, 68
continuous assessment 150
contractions 137, 138
conversational chains 85–6
corrections 34–7
  peer 35
  positive 34, 35
  procedure 34–5
  self 35
  timing of 34
  ways of making 35–7
course book 38–40

cues 69
cultural differences 12–13

debate and discussion 97–8, 103
  when using text 117, 118, 119
diagnostic tests 144, 145
dialogue 117–19, 153, 161–2
disappearing dialogues 76
discipline 26
drawing from descriptions 98–9
drilling 68–74, 89
  back chaining 70
  choral 68–70
  and cues 69
  interest and realism 69

elicitation 19, 58–60
errors 14, 34–5, 36, 37
  in Production phase 90, 91, 92, 94
examinations 7, 15
  see also tests and testing

factual text 114–17, 161
finger correction 36
fluency 7–8, 19, 37, 89, 90–106, 112
  and activities 90, 93–106, 159–60
  and choice of topic 92–3
fluency phase *see* Production phase
form filling 78
formal language 64–5, 88–9
free phase *see* Production phase
functional language 59, 159
  Practice phase 81–9
  presenting 63–6
    and levels of formality 64–5
    through listening 65–6
    through mime and puppets 63–4
    through reading 64–5

games and game boards 41, 86, 87
grammar 5, 20, 59
  controlled practice stage 68–77
    activities 71–7
    drilling 68–74
  guided practice stage 77–81
  presenting 60–3
    through comparison 61
    directly 61
    indirectly 62
    through pictures and objects 62
    through previous knowledge 62–3
    through situations 62
    through text 61
    when using text 111, 112

group work 27–30
  and fluency activities 92
  and practice phase 67, 68, 71
  responsibilities within 29–30, 37
  in teams 49–50
  and warmers 46, 47–9
guessing games 76–7
guided stage 37, 67, 77–81, 82–9, 158

ice-breakers, *see* warmers
idioms 60
information gap activities 69, 72–4, 79–80,
    88, 121, 153
information sharing 95–7
informing 147
interactive patterns 26–30, 32, 89
  group work 27–30
  new 29
  pair work 27–9
  testing of 147, 152–4
  variation within 31
  whole-class work 27
interest 16–17, 92–3
International Phonetic Alphabet (IPA)
    126
interrupting 84
intonation 57, 140–3

jazz chant 139–40
'jigsaw' groups 96

Kim's game 76

language
  experimentation with 6
  and poetry 121, 123
  practice in 7
  and real-life situations 7
  in use 5
  when using dialogue 119
  when using text 111–12, 116–17
  and young learners 10–11
language item 18
language skills integration 20–2
learners 9–11
  adult learners 9, 126
  personal differences 13–14
  young learners 10–11, 125
learning activities, *see* activities
learning contexts 8–9
less-controlled stage, *see* guided stage
lesson organization 18–23
  and activities 22–3
  language skills integration 20–2

lesson organization (*continued*)
  PPP model 18–20
  see also classroom organization
lesson planning 25

marking 148–9
  marking scheme 148
  rating scales 148–50
'messenger' process 96–7
mistakes, *see* errors
monitors 26
motivation 6, 8–9, 16–17
  improvement in 14

names of students 26, 45
narrative text 109–14, 160–1
noise 26, 29, 30–1
note making 14

pair work 27–9, 67, 68, 92
  and warmers 46–7
phrases 60
  useful 31, 33
placement tests 144, 145
poems 120–3, 162
posters 41, 51–3
PPP model 18–20, 56
  effectiveness of 19–20
  and language skills integration 20–2
Practice phase 19, 25, 67–89
  activities for 71–89
  and errors 34, 35–7
  and formal language 88–9
  and functional language 81–9
  grammar 68–81, 111, 112
  stages of 67–81
    controlled stage 19, 67, 68–77, 81–2,
      158
    guided stage 37, 67, 77–81, 82–9,
      158
  vocabulary 68–81, 112
  when using text 111–12
Presentation phase 19, 24–5, 56–66
  and errors 34
  of functional language 63–6
  of grammar 60–3
  important features 56–7
  and language context 57
  and pronunciation 57
  stages 58–60
  of vocabulary 60
  when using dialogue 119
  when using text 110, 116
presentations 100–3

problem solving 97–100
Production phase 19, 20, 25, 89, 90–106
  choice of topic 93
  and errors 34, 37
  and fluency activity management 90,
    93–106
  preparation and support for 91–2
  using texts 112–14, 117
  when using dialogue 119
proficiency tests 144, 145
progress tests 144
projects 100–3
pronunciation 57, 124–43
  activities 127–30, 132–3, 134–6,
    138–40, 141–3, 162–3
  and age of learners 125–6
  defined 124
  important elements 125
  sound recognition 125
  see also sounds
public speaking 102–3
puppets 43, 63–4

questionnaires 74–5, 88, 95–6

rating scales 148–50
reading 64–5, 116
relevance of topic 92–3
repetition 7, 20
  drills 19, 71
resources 1
responsibilities in group work 29–30, 37
role play 103–6, 112, 119
roles
  social 12–13
  of teacher 24–5
  within groups 29–30, 37, 92
routines and signals 25–6
rules
  for classroom management 26
  for speaking 12–13

sentence formation 80–1
sentence stress 133–6
  practice 134–6
  recognition 133–4
shyness 67
silence 16
social roles 12–13
sounds 124
  in connected speech 136–40
  practice 129–30
  recognition 127–9
  stress, *see* word stress

speaking
  importance of 5–6
  preparation for 16, 45–55
  reasons for practice 6
  testing skills 144–54
  and written examinations 15
spinner 86, 87
starters, *see* warmers
storage of teaching aids 41–2
stress
  in sentences, *see* sentence stress
  on words, *see* word stress
substitution drills 72, 73, 88
supportive atmosphere 14, 67, 150

target language 18
teacher's role 24–5
teaching aids 38–44
  board 40
  course book 38–40
  making 40–2
  storing 41–2, 44
team work 49–50
  see also group work
tenses 77–8
tests and testing 2, 7, 15, 144–54
  areas tested 146–8
  assessing and marking 148–50
  of communication skills 148
  guidelines for 145
  hearing and repeating 150–1
  of information giving 151–2
  of interactions 147, 152–4
  organization of 146
  suggestions for 150–4
  types of tests 144–5
text in speaking activities 107–23
  dialogue speaking activities 117–19,
    161–2
  factual text sample activities 114–17,
    161
  narrative text sample activities 109–14,
    160–1

poems 120–3
reasons for use 107–8
types of 108
writing text onto board 108
topics
  acceptability 93
  interest and relevance 92–3

understanding 110–11

vocabulary 5, 20, 59, 91
  controlled practice stage 68–77
    activities 71–7
    drilling 68–74
  guided practice stage 77–81
  presenting 60
  and repetition drills 71
  when using text 110, 112

warmers 45–55
  for groups 47–9
  listed 157–8
  for moving around the classroom 53–4
  organizing 45–6
  for pairs 46–9
  for teams 49
  uses of 45
  when using dialogue 118
  when using text 110, 116
  for whole class 50–5
    circle games 50–1
    involve student movement 53–4
    using blackboard/posters 51–3, 54–5
weak forms of words 137
whole-class work 27
word order 80–1
word stress 130–3
  practice activities 133
  recognition activities 132
writing activities 95, 113

young learners 10–11

ESSENTIAL SPEAKING SKILLS